Happy Cooking!

SANJEEV KAPOOR'S
100 FAVOURITE
HAND-PICKED RECIPES

SANJEEV KAPOOR'S
100 FAVOURITE
HAND-PICKED RECIPES

In association with Alyona Kapoor

PopulaR prakashan

www.popularprakashan.com

Published by

POPULAR PRAKASHAN PVT. LTD.

301, Mahalaxmi Chambers

22, Bhulabhai Desai Road

Mumbai - 400 026

for Khana Khazana Publications Pvt. Ltd.

(4376)

ISBN: 978-81-7991-628-5

Cover and channel advertising pages:

Fuschiant Graphic and Web Designs

Inside pages design and layout: Pratibha Gurnani Creative

Photography: Mangesh Parab, Alim Bolar, Bharat Bhirangi

and Swapnil Naik

Food Stylist: Anupa Das

PRINTED IN INDIA

By Rave India

A-27, Naraina Industrial Area, Phase II

New Delhi 110028

For my fans, viewers and loved ones…
a piece from my heart preserved for posterity.

author's note

I have lost count of the number of times I have been asked to list my favourite recipes. I have no doubt that the lists have differed each time, as when it comes to food it is hard to restrict oneself to just a few. Besides, one's mood, a recent discovery, a new experience, a renewed acquaintance with an old favourite, they all shape the list.

This is the current list of one hundred of my favourite recipes, foods that I not only love to eat but also love to cook! Needless to say, they are the first among equals, for like any parent I am loathe to name a favourite child, each one being special in their own way!

That being said, let me welcome you to my world which revolves around FOOD, FOOD and more food. This book of favourites has been published to coincide with the launch of my 24-hour food channel – the first of its kind in India. The channel will celebrate the diversity of the culinary traditions and practices of our country, and explore the cuisines of the world. Many of the dishes feature on my list of favourites and will be featured on the programmes as well.

We are a nation obsessed with food. Food plays a starring role at every festival and occasion, in every rite and every ritual. From infancy to maturity, food is the language of love. And like love, it knows no bounds – it grows and blossoms. While our constantly evolving food habits and tastes are rooted in our home kitchens, they are increasingly responsive to the myriad new culinary styles, flavours and ingredients we encounter in books, restaurants, on our travels and now, even on TV.

FOODFOOD, the 24-hour TV food channel will give you the opportunity to watch me cook my favourite dishes and I am sure they will become your favourites too. Let the aromas of a 100 dishes from all over the world perfume your home and fill you with a passion and hunger for more.

Happy Cooking and Happy Viewing!

Sanjeev Kapoor

Sanjeev Kapoor's 100 Favourite Hand-Picked Recipes celebrates the launch of the new TV channel FOODFOOD, India's first food and food lifestyle media brand, the brainchild of renowned Master Chef Sanjeev Kapoor. The only 24x7 Hindi channel in Indian television history that is solely devoted to cuisine, FOODFOOD features programmes that are great to watch and great to learn from.

Sanjeev Kapoor's Kitchen gives you a close peek into the 'hows' and 'whats' of cooking. Chef Kapoor teaches you how to whip up simple, interesting and tasty dishes.

Watch an enthralling, nail-biting contest in **Chef Se Hai Muqabala** as professional chefs compete against everyday cooks to cook up an extraordinary meal.

Firangi Tadka is all about international cuisine with a desi touch. Cordon Bleu chef Chinu shows you how to cook exotic dishes with Indian ingredients.

Health Mange More gives all your meals a healthy, nutritious twist, with guilt-free recipes for delicious dishes provided by chefs and nutritionists working in tandem.

Quick cooking is the name of the game in **Sirf 30 Minute** as four renowned chefs show you how to make a full-course meal in less than half an hour. And the dishes are from every region in India and to suit every taste.

Toh, chalein kitchen mein?

contents

Beverages

Black Grape Sherbet	14
Virgin Piña Colada	16
Kokum and Anar Slush	18
Tropical Fruit and Nut Smoothie	19
Coffee Ambrosia	20

Soups

Mushroom Cappuccino	22
Cream of Asparagus and Almond Soup	24
Minestrone Toscano with Pesto Croûte	26
Chicken Noodle Soup	27
Prawn Ball Soup	28

Salads

Grape and Walnut Raita	30
Vegetable Ribbon Salad	32
Chilled Melon Ball Salad	34
Fruit and Capsicum Kachumber	35
Caesar Salad	36
Rojak	38
Tropical Chicken and Farfalle Salad	40
Coriander Prawns and Mango Salad	41
Warm Thai Noodle and Papaya Salad	42

Snacks, Starters

Kanchipuram Idli	44
Spring Dosa	46
Phal-Subz Seekh	47
Paneer ke Tinke	48
Tandoori Subz Shashlik	50
Papad Paneer Rolls	52
Bhakarwadi Chaat	53
Katori Chaat	54
Tiranga Paneer Tikka	56
Baby Corn Satay	57
Vegetable Tempura	58
Spicy Moroccan Wraps	60
Golden Bags	62
Dhaniya Adrak Champe	64
Mutton Shammi Kababs	65
Salt and Pepper Prawns	66
Chao Tom – Prawn on a Sugarcane Stick	68
Kadai Prawns with Roasted Pepper Jam	70
Fish Cakes with Cucumber Relish	72
Chettinad Kozhi Varuval	73
Yakitori Chicken with Spring Onions	74

Main Courses

Baghare Baingan	76
Dahiwale Amrud	78
Dahi Papad ki Sabzi	79
Aviyal	80
Achaari Gobhi	82
Capsicum Kayras	83
Chole Dhania Masala	84
Shaam Savera	86
Ekadashi Jeera Aloo	87
Bhare Baghare Tamatar	88
Chicken Teriyaki with Black Grapes	90
Green Chilli Chicken	92
Butter Chicken	93
Patrani Machchi	94
Malabar Prawn Curry	95
Nalli Nihari	96
Braised Lamb with Spinach and Leeks	98
Stir-fried Tofu with Asian Greens	99
Ratatouille	100

Pan-fried Mushrooms	101
Frittata with Caramalised Onions and Roasted Peppers	102
Thai Green Curry with Vegetables	104

Rice, Noodles, Pasta

Kaju Moti Pulao	106
Jodhpuri Vegetable Pulao	107
Erra Saadam	108
Handi Biryani	110
Kachche Gosht ki Biryani	111
Mushroom Pot Rice	112
Shanghai Stewed Noodles	113
Seafood Pad Thai	114
Spicy Chicken Fried Rice with Crispy Basil Leaves	116
Oodles of Noodles	117
Penne with Creamy Pesto and Cherry Tomatoes	118
Cheesy Macaroni	120

Accompaniments

Sindhi Dal	122
Dal Maharani	123
Methiwali Arhar Dal	124
Dal Lucknowi	126
Maa Chole di Dal	127
Bhinda ni Kadhi	128
Aamras ki Kadhi	129
Appam	130
Sheermal	132
Moong Dal Puri	133
Taftan	134
Murgh Missi Roti	136
Tamatar ki Chutney	137
Teekha Nimbu Achaar	138
Spinach Chutney	140
Keri ki Launjee	142

Sweets, Desserts

Kesari Indrayani	144
Saeb aur Sooji ka Halwa	146
Mysore Paak	147
Balushahi	148
Khubani ka Meetha	150
Gajar aur Khajur ka Halwa	151
Mango Cheesecake	152
Black Forest Gâteau	154
Strawberry Panna Cotta	155
Tiramisù	156

Annexure	**158**
Glossary	**160**

| beverages | soups | salads |

01

black grape
sherbet

This exotic drink of luscious black grapes tinged with earthy spices, is the perfect thirst-quencher on a hot summer's day.

ingredients:

- 4 cups black grape juice • ¾ teaspoon cumin seeds • ½ teaspoon carom seeds • 1 teaspoon fennel seeds • 3 teaspoons black salt • 1½ tablespoons Tamarind Pulp (page 158) • Crushed ice

method:

1. Dry-roast the cumin seeds, carom seeds and fennel seeds, and grind with the black salt to a fine powder.

2. Pour the black grape juice into a jug; add the ground spices and tamarind pulp, and mix well.

3. Add the crushed ice and mix. Pour into individual glasses and serve chilled.

02
virgin piña colada

A sip of this silky, smooth blend of tropical flavours transports one instantly to hot sandy beaches fringed with cool green coconut palms.

ingredients:

- 1¾ cups unsweetened pineapple juice
- 8 tablespoons thick coconut milk
- 8 tablespoons grated tender coconut
- 2 cups vanilla ice cream
- 8 tablespoons chopped pineapple chunks
- 16-20 tinned cherries, drained
- Crushed ice, as required

method:

1. Blend the pineapple juice, coconut milk, coconut, ice cream and ice till smooth.

2. Pour into individual glasses.

3. Serve immediately, decorated with pineapple chunks and cherries.

03
kokum and anar slush

This icy sour-sweet deep magenta concoction,
sprinkled with ruby red pomegranates is a jewel of
a drink and always a great hit with family and friends.

• 1⅓ cups *kokum* syrup • 4 tablespoons pomegranate kernels • 2 teaspoons roasted cumin powder
• 2 teaspoons black salt • 8 tablespoons sugar • 4 cups crushed ice

method:

1. Process the *kokum* syrup, roasted cumin powder, black salt, sugar and the crushed ice in a blender until slushy.

2. Pour into individual glasses, decorate with a sprinkling of pomegranate kernels and serve.

04
tropical fruit and nut smoothie

The flavours and colours of summer in a glass - my favourite pick-me-up and cool-me-down.

ingredients:

- 1 apple, peeled, cored and sliced • 2 ripe mangoes, chopped • 2 bananas, sliced • ½ cup golden raisins • 12-16 pistachios, chopped • Crushed ice

method:

1. Place the prepared fruit in a freezer till frozen.

2. Process the frozen apple, mangoes and bananas with golden raisins and crushed ice in a blender. Pour into individual glasses.

3. Serve, garnished with the chopped pistachios.

05
coffee ambrosia

This is one for those relaxed moments after a meal with friends. A hot coffee beverage, laced with a creamy liqueur - guaranteed to make you feel warm all over. The ice cream will add a delicious cold contrast.

ingredients:

- 4 teaspoons instant coffee powder ● 3 cups milk ● 4 tablespoons sugar ● 4 small scoops vanilla ice cream
- 4 tablespoons Advocaat (liqueur)

method:

1. Heat the milk in a non-stick pan and set aside.

2. To make the coffee, combine the coffee powder and sugar in a large bowl. Add two to three tablespoons of water and whisk for six to eight minutes till the mixture changes colour and turns creamy.

3. Pour the mixture into four large cups. Strain the milk and pour into the cups till three-fourth full and stir gently.

4. Gently place a scoop of ice cream on the coffee in each cup. Drizzle a tablespoon of Advocaat over the ice cream and serve immediately.

06

mushroom cappuccino

I enjoy the look of surprised delight on unsuspecting guests' faces when they take a sip of what turns out to be thick creamy mushroom soup instead of coffee!

ingredients:

• 15 large fresh button mushrooms, thickly sliced • 2 cups milk, chilled • 1 tablespoon butter • 1 bay leaf
• 1 small onion, chopped • 4-6 garlic cloves, chopped • 4 cups Vegetable Stock (page 159) • Salt to taste
• ¼ teaspoon white pepper powder • ¾ cup cream • 1 teaspoon cinnamon powder

method:

1. Melt the butter in a heavy-bottomed non-stick pan. Add the bay leaf, onion and garlic, and sauté for two to three minutes or till the onion is translucent.

2. Add the mushrooms and sauté for one minute. Add one cup of vegetable stock and cook for five more minutes. Remove from the heat and cool. Remove the bay leaf and discard.

3. Make a purée of the cooked mushrooms and add the remaining vegetable stock. Return to the heat and bring to a boil. Add salt and white pepper powder, lower the heat and simmer for two to three minutes.

4. Stir in the cream and remove from the heat. Pour the soup into individual cups and keep warm.

5. Pour the chilled milk into a chilled bowl. Beat with a fork till it develops a thick froth. Collect the froth with a ladle and place on the hot mushroom soup giving it a cappuccino effect.

6. Sprinkle cinnamon powder and serve immediately.

chef's tip:

Use milk with a high fat content for a thick froth.

07
cream of asparagus and almond soup

This pale green pool of perfection sets the right tone at the start of an elegant meal.

ingredients:

- 300 grams asparagus •10-12 almonds •Salt to taste •2 tablespoons butter •1 medium onion, chopped
- 2 tablespoons refined flour •2½ cups Vegetable Stock (page 159) •4-5 black peppercorns, crushed
- 2 cups milk

method:

1. Trim the asparagus, discarding the woody part of the stem. Cut the remainder into short lengths, reserving a few tips for garnishing. Blanch the reserved tips in boiling salted water for one or two minutes. Drain and refresh in cold water.

2. Blanch the remaining asparagus in boiling water for two to three minutes. Drain and refresh in cold water. Purée the asparagus in a blender.

3. Broil or dry-roast the almonds over medium heat till the skins change colour slightly. Remove from the heat, cool and cut into slivers.

4. Melt the butter in a non-stick pan and add the onion. Sauté over a low heat until soft. Stir in the flour and cook for one minute, then gradually add the stock and whisk so that no lumps are formed.

5. Bring the mixture to a boil. Lower the heat and simmer for two to three minutes until thickened. Stir in the asparagus purée, salt and crushed peppercorns.

6. Add the milk and simmer for two to three minutes, stirring continuously.

7. Serve hot, garnished with the blanched asparagus tips and almond slivers.

08
minestrone toscano with pesto croûte

Sprawled in front of the TV with a bowl of this chunky soup and some crusty bread - my favourite Me Time.

ingredients:

• 2 tablespoons macaroni • 3 cups Vegetable Stock (page 159) • 1 medium potato, cut into small pieces • 1 medium carrot, cut into small pieces • 3-4 French beans, cut into small pieces • Salt to taste • ½ teaspoon white pepper powder • ¼ small cabbage, shredded • 1 medium zucchini, cut into small pieces • 2 tablespoons Tomato Concassé (page 159) • ½ cup tomato purée • 1½ tablespoons olive oil • 6-8 garlic cloves, chopped • 1 medium onion, chopped • ¼ teaspoon crushed dried oregano • 10-12 fresh basil leaves, roughly torn • ⅓ cup grated Parmesan cheese

method:

1. Bring the vegetable stock to a boil in a deep non-stick pan. Add the macaroni and potato, and cook over a moderate heat for one minute.

2. Add the carrot and French beans, and continue to cook for a while. Add the salt and white pepper powder, and mix. Add the cabbage, zucchini, tomato concassé and tomato purée.

3. In the meanwhile, heat the olive oil in a non-stick pan. Add the garlic and onion, and sauté till translucent. Add the oregano and continue to sauté. Add to the soup and stir to mix.

4. Add the basil and continue to simmer till the vegetables are cooked. Sprinkle the Parmesan cheese and serve piping hot with Pesto Croûte or Garlic Bread (see below).

Pesto Croûte
Process 1 cup fresh basil, 5-6 garlic cloves, ¼ cup pine nuts, salt to taste, and 2 tablespoons olive oil in a blender till smooth. Add ⅓ cup Parmesan cheese and process again. Spread on toasted bread.

Garlic Bread
Preheat the oven to 200C/400F/Gas Mark 6. Cream 4 tablespoons butter till smooth; add 2 teaspoons garlic paste and 5-6 crushed peppercorns. Slit a French loaf diagonally 2 inches apart and spread the garlic butter between the slits. Wrap the loaf in aluminium foil and heat in the oven for 5 to 8 minutes.

09
chicken noodle soup

Our children describe their favourite soup as 'slurrpalicious', and that is exactly what it is!

ingredients:

●300 grams rice noodles or rice vermicelli ●2 fresh red chillies, seeded and sliced ●2 tablespoons soy sauce ●1¼ cups bean sprouts, blanched ●1 medium onion, sliced ●White pepper powder to taste ●10-12 fresh basil leaves ●2 tablespoons chopped fresh coriander ●1 lemon, cut into wedges

Broth
●10 cups Chicken Stock (page 159) ●500 grams boneless chicken, cubed ●1 inch cinnamon ●2-3 spring onion green stalks, sliced ●1 inch ginger, crushed ●2 teaspoons sugar ●Salt to taste ●2 tablespoons fish sauce

method:

1. Place the sliced red chillies in a bowl and add the soy sauce. Set aside.

2. For the broth, pour the chicken stock into a deep non-stick pan. Add the chicken cubes, cinnamon, spring onions, ginger, sugar and salt, and bring to a boil over high heat. Lower heat and simmer for forty-five minutes, skimming the scum off as it rises to the surface.

3. Add the fish sauce and remove from heat. Remove the chicken with a slotted spoon and set aside to cool. Strain the broth and keep warm over very low heat.

4. Boil plenty of water in a deep non-stick pan. Add the noodles and blanch for about five minutes or until they soften. If using vermicelli it will take around two minutes. Drain and rinse in cold water. Drain again thoroughly and set aside.

5. When the chicken cools completely, shred into thin strips.

6. Place the noodles/vermicelli in individual serving bowls, top with bean sprouts, shredded chicken and onion. Pour the hot broth into the bowls. Sprinkle with white pepper powder; garnish with the basil and chopped coriander. Serve piping hot, with the lemon wedges and the bowl of red chillies in soy sauce on the side.

10
prawn ball soup

Spongy dumplings packed with flavour, swimming in a clear broth are a particular family favourite, especially with Alyona, who loves seafood.

ingredients:

- 250 grams prawns, shelled, deveined and minced • 3-4 slices tinned bamboo shoots • Salt to taste
- Black pepper powder to taste • 1 tablespoon cornflour • 1 egg white, beaten • 1 tablespoon olive oil
- 1 inch ginger, chopped • 5-6 medium fresh button mushrooms, sliced • 5-6 black peppercorns, crushed
- 4 cups Chicken Stock (page 159) • 10-12 fresh spinach leaves, shredded • 2-3 spring onion green stalks

method:

1. Boil the bamboo shoots in two cups of water for three to four minutes. Drain and cut into strips. Set aside.

2. Add the salt and black pepper powder to the minced prawns and mix. Add the cornflour and egg white, and mix well. Shape teaspoonfuls of the mixture into small balls.

3. Heat the oil in a non-stick pan and sauté the ginger for half a minute. Add the bamboo shoots, mushrooms, crushed peppercorns, salt and chicken stock, and bring to a boil.

4. Add the prawn balls and cook for two to three minutes. Add the shredded spinach and simmer for one minute.

5. Serve hot, garnished with spring onion greens.

11

grape and walnut raita

I love the cool contrast this salad makes to heavy *biryani* and rice dishes. The crisp grapes and crunchy walnuts add a delightful texture to the flavoured yogurt.

ingredients:

• 25-30 green grapes, seeded and halved • ¼ cup walnut kernels, chopped • 2 cups yogurt • Salt to taste • 1½ teaspoons sugar • ½ teaspoon roasted cumin powder • 2 tablespoons chopped fresh mint • A large pinch of red chilli powder

method:

1. Whisk the yogurt in a large bowl with the salt, sugar and cumin powder.

2. Add the grapes, walnuts and mint, and fold in gently. Place in a refrigerator to chill.

3. Sprinkle the chilli powder and serve.

12
vegetable ribbon salad

This is the way I like my vegetables – raw and coated with a tangy dressing. Healthy *bhi*, tasty *bhi*!

ingredients:

- 1 medium zucchini, trimmed • 2 medium carrots, trimmed • 2 medium cucumbers, trimmed • Salt to taste
- 5 medium black olives, stoned and sliced

Dressing
- 2 tablespoons vinegar • 1 tablespoon soy sauce • 1 teaspoon brown sugar • ¼ teaspoon red chilli flakes
- 3-4 fresh basil leaves • Salt to taste

method:

1. Cut the zucchini, carrots and cucumbers lengthways into thin ribbons with a potato peeler or a manual slicer. Sprinkle a little salt and set aside for five minutes.

2. Process the vinegar, soy sauce, brown sugar, chilli flakes, basil leaves and salt to make a coarse paste in a blender. Transfer to a bowl.

3. Squeeze the cut vegetables gently to remove excess liquid.

4. Add the vegetables to the dressing in the bowl and toss well.

5. Serve, garnished with olive slices.

chef's tip:

Serve the salad immediately as zucchini tends to become soggy.

13
chilled melon ball salad

The explosion of flavours as I bite into the melon, recreates for me memories of delicious childhood encounters with enormous slices of ruby red watermelon, the juices running down my chin. Give me more!

ingredients:

● ¼ watermelon ● 1 medium musk melon

Dressing
● 1½ teaspoons lemon juice ● 2 tablespoons orange juice ● 3-4 black peppercorns, crushed ● 1 tablespoon roughly torn fresh mint ● Salt to taste ● Black salt to taste

method:

1. Using a Parisienne scoop (melon baller) scoop out small balls from the watermelon. Discard all the seeds.

2. Cut the musk melon in half. Scoop out small balls from the centre, leaving a thick shell around. Discard all the seeds. Reserve the melon shells.

3. Place the melon balls in a refrigerator to chill thoroughly.

4. Mix together all the ingredients for the dressing. Pour over the melon balls and toss gently once or twice to mix. Spoon into the melon shells and serve immediately.

chef's tip:

The melon shells can be given a decorative zigzag edge using a small sharp knife. You can also serve the salad in a bowl.

14

fruit and capsicum kachumber

This is a *kachumber* with attitude! The fruit and vegetables vie for attention on the palate, every mouthful a tug-of-war of flavours.

ingredients:

- 2 medium apples, cored and sliced thinly • 2 medium oranges • 12-15 seedless green grapes, halved
- 1 medium green capsicum, cut into strips • 1 tablespoon lemon juice • 1 medium cucumber, sliced thinly
- 2 medium tomatoes, seeded and cut into strips • 2 spring onions, sliced thinly

Dressing
- 1 tablespoon chopped fresh coriander • 8-10 fresh mint leaves, roughly torn • 2 green chillies, chopped
- 1½ teaspoons *chaat masala* • Salt to taste • 1 tablespoon lemon juice

method:

1. Sprinkle the lemon juice over the apple slices to prevent discolouration.

2. Peel the oranges and separate the segments. Remove the seeds and cut each segment in half.

3. For the dressing, mix together the chopped coriander, mint leaves, green chillies, *chaat masala*, salt and lemon juice.

4. Toss the fruit and vegetables in the dressing and serve chilled.

15
caesar salad

This is my favourite version of the world-famous salad. I have a particular fondness for it as it was served in my friend's restaurant in Wellington, New Zealand.

ingredients:

• 2 thick slices of bread, cut into 1-inch pieces • 1 tablespoon oil • 135 grams iceberg lettuce • 100 grams lollo rosso or iceberg lettuce • 5-6 basil leaves • 100 grams Parmesan cheese, shaved or grated

Dressing
• 2 eggs • Sea salt to taste • 2 garlic cloves • 3-4 peppercorns • 1 teaspoon Worcestershire sauce • 1 teaspoon French mustard paste • 2 tablespoons extra virgin olive oil

method:

1. For the dressing, boil sufficient water in a non-stick pan; add the eggs and boil for four minutes only.

2. Crush the sea salt, garlic and peppercorns with a mortar and pestle. Transfer to a bowl. Add the Worcestershire sauce and mustard paste, and mix well.

3. Break the lightly boiled eggs and add to the mixture along with the olive oil.

4. For the salad, heat the oil in a non-stick pan; add the bread cubes and sauté till slightly crisp and browned at the edges. Remove and set aside.

5. Wash and dry the lettuce leaves; tear them roughly and place in a large bowl. Tear basil leaves and add to the lettuce. Add the cheese.

6. Add the fried bread and toss to mix. Pour the dressing over the salad and toss lightly. Serve immediately.

16
rojak

Street food-turned-haute cuisine is how I would describe this popular Malaysian salad.

ingredients:

•1½ fresh pineapple, cut into ½-inch cubes •1 small yam, cut into ½-inch cubes and boiled •1 cucumber, cut into ½-inch cubes •3 tablespoons brown sugar •¼ cup tamarind juice •3 fresh red chillies, seeded and chopped

method:

1. Mix together the brown sugar, tamarind juice and red chillies in a small bowl.

2. Place the pineapple, yam and cucumber in a bowl. Add the dressing and toss well to mix.

3. Serve immediately.

17

tropical chicken and farfalle salad

Who needs mayo when you have a flavourful, light dressing with which to drench this colourful chicken-pasta combo?

ingredients:

● 200 grams boneless chicken, boiled and shredded ● 1 cup farfalle (bow-tie pasta) ● 1 medium tomato, cut into ½-inch cubes ● 1 medium carrot, cut into ½-inch cubes ● ½ medium green capsicum, cut into ½-inch cubes ● ½ medium yellow capsicum, cut into ½-inch cubes ● 8-10 olives, stoned and sliced into rings

Dressing
● 4-5 garlic cloves, chopped ● 2 inches celery stalk, finely chopped ● ½ teaspoon red chilli flakes ● 2-3 tablespoons lemon juice ● Salt to taste ● 2 teaspoons finely chopped fresh parsley

method:

1. Boil three cups of water in a deep non-stick pan. Add the pasta and boil till *al dente* (cooked, but firm to the bite). Drain and refresh in cold water.

2. To make the dressing, mix together the garlic, celery, chilli flakes, lemon juice, salt and parsley in a bowl.

3. In a large bowl, mix together the pasta, chicken, tomato, carrot, green and yellow capsicums and olives.

4. Pour the dressing over and toss to mix. Serve immediately.

18

coriander prawns and mango salad

The coriander chutney gives the prawns zing, and the mango adds flair. Which is why I sometimes refer to this salad as 'Punch and Panache'!

ingredients:

• ¾ cup small prawns, peeled and deveined • ½ cup Green Chutney (page 158) • 1 small unripe mango, peeled and cut into thin strips • 2 medium tomatoes • 1 teaspoon mustard paste • Salt to taste • 4-5 tablespoons sugar • ½ teaspoon black peppercorns, crushed • 1 teaspoon lemon juice • 4-5 iceberg lettuce leaves, placed in iced water

method:

1. Halve the tomatoes, remove seeds and cut into strips.

2. Marinate the prawns in the green chutney for about fifteen minutes.

3. Heat a non-stick *tawa* and roast the prawns till tender.

4. Mix together the unripe mango strips, tomato strips, mustard paste, salt, sugar, crushed peppercorns, lemon juice and one tablespoon of water.

5. Add the grilled prawns and toss to mix. Serve on a bed of iceberg lettuce.

19

warm thai noodle and papaya salad

There is a reason why this mélange of oriental flavours has made it to my list of favourites – the tantalizing medley of colours, textures and flavours, plus the unusual fact that unlike most salads, it is served warm and straight off a wok.

ingredients:

● 100 grams cellophane or glass noodles ● ½ medium unripe green papaya, sliced ● 3 tablespoons oil ● 4 garlic cloves, chopped ● ½ medium green capsicum, cut into ½-inch pieces ● 1 inch celery stalk, sliced ● 2 tablespoons fish sauce (optional) ● Salt to taste ● ¼ teaspoon white pepper powder ● ½ cup roasted peanuts, crushed ● 1 cup bean sprouts ● 1 tablespoon lemon juice ● 1 tablespoon chopped fresh coriander

method:

1. Soak the noodles in hot water for a few minutes. Drain and refresh in cold water. Add one tablespoon of oil and toss to coat the noodles with the oil.

2. Heat the remaining oil in a non-stick wok. Add the garlic and stir-fry for a few minutes or until light golden brown. Add the papaya slices, capsicum and celery, and stir-fry for a minute.

3. Add the noodles and toss to mix. Season with the fish sauce, salt and white pepper powder. Remove from the heat.

4. Add the crushed peanuts and bean sprouts. Add the lemon juice, mix well and serve warm, garnished with the chopped coriander.

| snacks | starters |

20
kanchipuram idli

Say 'Kanchipuram' and Alyona has visions of rich silk, but I can only think of those soft gold discs, nestling alongside a rugged mound of coconut chutney on a glossy green banana leaf.

ingredients:

● 1 cup short grained rice ● ½ cup skinless split black gram ● ¾ teaspoon fenugreek seeds ● 1 teaspoon turmeric powder ● 30 black peppercorns, coarsely crushed ● 2 teaspoons split Bengal gram ● A pinch of asafoetida ● 1 cup yogurt ● ½ cup pure ghee ● Salt to taste ● A few tender banana leaves

To Serve
● *Sambhar* and Coconut Chutney (page 158)

method:

1. Soak the rice and black gram with the fenugreek seeds in three cups of water, for three to four hours. Drain and grind to a smooth paste with half a cup of water to make a thick batter of pouring consistency. Transfer to a deep bowl.

2. Add the turmeric powder, peppercorns, Bengal gram, asafoetida, yogurt, ghee and salt. Mix well and leave to ferment overnight.

3. Whip the batter well, add one-fourth cup of water to adjust the consistency. The batter should be fairly thick.

4. Heat sufficient water in a steamer. Line the *idli* cups with the banana leaves and pour the batter into them. Place in the steamer and steam for about twenty minutes or till risen and fluffy.

5. Serve hot with *sambhar* and coconut chutney.

21
spring dosa

This is my salute to street food vendors who are innovative and always have their finger on the pulse of local tastes.

ingredients:

●2 cups ready-made *dosa* batter ●2 tablespoons + 2 teaspoons oil ●1 medium onion, thinly sliced ●2 medium carrots, grated ●1 medium green capsicum, cut into thin strips ●1 cup finely shredded cabbage ●½ tablespoon light soy sauce ●½ teaspoon white pepper powder ●5 tablespoons Sichuan Sauce (page 159) ●Salt to taste ●½ cup bean sprouts ●½ cup finely chopped spring onion greens ●2 teaspoons butter

method:

1. To make the filling, heat two tablespoons oil in a non-stick wok; add the onion, carrots and capsicum, and stir-fry for half a minute. Add the cabbage and continue to stir-fry for one minute longer. Add the soy sauce, white pepper powder, one tablespoon Sichuan sauce and salt.

2. Add the bean sprouts and spring onion greens, and stir-fry for about half a minute. Set the mixture aside to cool completely and divide into four equal portions.

3. Heat a non-stick griddle, flat frying pan or a *dosa tawa* on medium heat for one or two minutes. Rub the *dosa tawa* with a lightly oiled cloth. Pour one-fourth cup of *dosa* batter into the pan and spread it evenly with the back of the ladle to make a nine-inch round *dosa*. Drizzle half a teaspoon of oil all around and cook over low heat for one minute.

4. Spread half a teaspoon of butter and one tablespoon of Sichuan sauce all over the *dosa*. Place one portion of the filling at one end of the *dosa* and gently roll it up. Continue to cook till the roll turns golden brown on all sides.

5. Cut diagonally into pieces and serve immediately.

22
phal-subz seekh

The fragrance wafting from these melt-in-the-mouth kababs, anointed with sandalwood and rose petals, is what makes them a particular favourite of mine.

ingredients:

• 2 large unripe bananas, halved • 200 grams fresh button mushrooms, chopped • 1 small carrot, grated • 4 broccoli florets, chopped • 2 medium potatoes, boiled, peeled and mashed • 5½ tablespoons butter • ¾ teaspoon carom seeds • ¾ tablespoon chopped fresh coriander • ¾ inch ginger, chopped • 1½ fresh red chillies, chopped • Salt to taste • 8 stoned prunes, chopped • ½ teaspoon black salt • ¾ teaspoon black pepper powder • ½ teaspoon green cardamom powder • A pinch of edible sandalwood powder • A pinch of dried rose petal powder • ½ cup breadcrumbs

method:

1. Cook the unpeeled bananas in four cups of water for fifteen minutes till tender. Drain and set aside to cool. Peel and grate the bananas.

2. Heat one and a half tablespoons of butter in a non-stick pan; add the carom seeds and sauté over medium heat for ten seconds. Add the mushrooms, carrot and broccoli, and sauté till the moisture evaporates. Add the chopped coriander, ginger, red chillies and salt. Stir, remove from heat and set aside to cool.

3. Preheat an oven to 180C/350F/Gas Mark 4.

4. Place the cooled mixture in a blender; add the mashed potato and banana, the prunes, black salt, pepper powder, cardamom powder, sandalwood powder, rose petal powder and breadcrumbs, and process till smooth.

5. Transfer the mixture to a bowl and divide into six equal portions.

6. Press each portion around a satay stick.

7. Grease a tray with a little butter and arrange the satay sticks on it. Brush with the remaining butter and cook in the preheated oven for six to seven minutes.

8. Gently slide the kababs from the satay sticks onto a plate, and cut each into four pieces and serve immediately.

23

paneer
ke tinke

Paneer is to Punjab what feta is to Greece. Every Punjab *da puttar* has a favourite *paneer* recipe, and this is one of mine.

ingredients:

● 300 grams cottage cheese, cut into 1-inch cubes ● 3 teaspoons oil ● 2 tablespoons gram flour ● ¾ cup drained (hung) yogurt ● 1 teaspoon roasted cumin powder ● 3-4 black peppercorns, crushed ● ½ teaspoon roasted crushed dried fenugreek leaves ● ½ teaspoon turmeric powder ● ½ teaspoon *garam masala* powder ● 5 teaspoons lemon juice ● Salt to taste ● A few saffron threads (optional) ● 1 medium onion, cut into 1-inch pieces, layers separated ● 1 medium green capsicum, cut into 1-inch pieces ● 1 medium red capsicum, cut into 1-inch pieces ● 6 satay sticks ● Mint Chutney (page 158), to serve

method:

1. Heat one teaspoon of oil in a non-stick pan and roast the gram flour on low heat till fragrant.

2. Place the yogurt, cumin powder, peppercorns, dried fenugreek leaves, turmeric powder, *garam masala* powder, lemon juice, salt and saffron in a bowl and mix well. Add the roasted gram flour and mix well. Add the cottage cheese cubes and toss gently. Set aside to marinate for ten to fifteen minutes.

3. Thread the ingredients in the following order onto the satay sticks: onion, cottage cheese, green capsicum, red capsicum, cottage cheese, onion. Heat a shallow non-stick pan; add the remaining oil and place the satay sticks on it. Cook on medium heat, turning the satay sticks from time to time so that the cottage cheese pieces are cooked evenly all around.

4. Serve hot with mint chutney.

24
tandoori subz shashlik

The pairing of sweet pineapple with piquant capsicum is a marriage made in heaven, or in this case a *tandoor*!

ingredients:

•200 grams pineapple, cut into 1½-inch cubes •2 medium green capsicum, cut into 1½-inch pieces •2 medium onions, cut into 1½-inch pieces •2 medium tomatoes, seeded and cut into 1½-inch pieces •Salt to taste •2 teaspoons red chilli powder •1½ teaspoons powdered dried fenugreek leaves •2 teaspoons *garam masala* powder •1 teaspoon *chaat masala* •2 tablespoons vinegar •1 tablespoon oil

method:

1. In a bowl, mix together the salt, chilli powder, powdered dried fenugreek leaves, *garam masala* powder, *chaat masala*, vinegar and oil. Add the pineapple and vegetables, and mix thoroughly. Set aside to marinate for one hour.

2. Thread the pineapple, capsicum, onion and tomato one after the other onto toothpicks. Pour the remaining marinade on top.

3. Heat a non-stick *tawa*, place the toothpicks on it and cook over medium heat, turning the toothpicks a few times so that the vegetables cook evenly on all sides. Cook till lightly-coloured.

4. Serve hot with a salad and chutney.

25

papad paneer rolls

A *pappadom* filled with promise, is how I think of these cone-shaped delights. A promise that has never yet been broken!

ingredients:

● 8 seven-inch *urad papad* ● 150 grams cottage cheese, cut into ½-inch cubes ● 1-2 green chillies, chopped ● ½ teaspoon red chilli powder ● ½ teaspoon cumin powder ● 1 teaspoon *chaat masala* ● 2 tablespoons chopped fresh coriander ● ½ inch ginger, chopped ● Salt to taste

method:

1. Mix together the cottage cheese, green chillies, chilli powder, cumin powder, *chaat masala*, chopped coriander, ginger and salt.

2. Cut each *papad* in half. Roast directly over an open flame or on a hot non-stick *tawa* and shape immediately into a cone.

3. Arrange the cones in a deep bowl and stuff them with the cottage cheese mixture.

4. Serve immediately.

26
bhakarwadi chaat

Here's where necessity gave birth to invention. A craving for *chaat* – something crisp, smothered with cool *dahi* and sloshes of hot and sweet chutneys – resulted in this impromptu snack, which has become a family favourite.

ingredients:

●1 cup mini *bhakarwadi* ●½ cup bean sprouts ●1 cup yogurt ●Salt to taste ●2 medium potatoes, boiled and finely chopped ●1 large onion, finely chopped ●5 tablespoons Green Chutney (page 158) ●3 tablespoons Date and Tamarind Chutney (page 158) ●1 teaspoon *chaat masala* ●¼ teaspoon red chilli powder ●1 teaspoon roasted cumin powder ●¼ cup nylon *sev* ●2 tablespoons chopped fresh coriander

method:

1. Cook the bean sprouts in one and a half cups of boiling salted water for two or three minutes. Drain, refresh in cold water and set aside.

2. Whisk the yogurt with salt and place in a refrigerator to chill for half an hour.

3. To prepare the *chaat*, arrange the *bhakarwadi* in a large serving plate; top with layers of bean sprouts, potatoes, onion and chilled yogurt.

4. Drizzle both the chutneys and sprinkle *chaat masala*, chilli powder, cumin powder and nylon *sev* over the yogurt.

5. Garnish with chopped coriander and serve immediately.

27

katori chaat

This is one of my guilty pleasures: deep-fried potato baskets, supporting a mountain of *chole*, with an avalanche of yogurt, streaked with rivulets of brown and green chutney, running down its sides.

ingredients:

Katori
- 5 medium potatoes • 2 tablespoons cornflour • Salt to taste • Oil for deep-frying

Filling
- 1 cup chickpeas, soaked • Salt to taste • 2 tea bags • 2 tablespoons ghee • 2 medium onions, chopped
- 1 teaspoon ginger paste • 1 teaspoon garlic paste • 4 tablespoons *chole masala* • ¾ cup tomato purée
- 4 tablespoons chopped fresh coriander

To Serve
- 4 tablespoons thick yogurt • 2 tablespoons Date and Tamarind Chutney (page 158) • 2 tablespoons Green Chutney (page 158) • 4 tablespoons *sev* • 2 tablespoons chopped fresh coriander

method:

1. Grate the potatoes coarsely and soak them in six cups of water for five minutes. Drain on absorbent paper. Transfer to a bowl, add the cornflour and a little salt and mix well. Divide into four portions.

2. Take two small strainers – one slightly larger than the other. Heat sufficient oil in a non-stick *kadai*. For each *katori*, layer the larger strainer with one portion of the grated potatoes. Place the other strainer over the potato layer and press lightly. Gently lower both the strainers together into the hot oil and deep-fry till the potatoes are golden. Drain on absorbent paper and set aside.

3. To make the *chole* (filling), drain the chickpeas, and place in a pressure cooker with three cups of water, salt and the tea bags. Pressure-cook till the pressure is released five to six times (five to six whistles) till the chickpeas are soft. Drain, reserving one-fourth cup of cooking liquid, and set aside.

4. Heat two tablespoons of ghee in a deep non-stick pan on medium heat; add the onions and sauté till golden. Add the ginger paste and garlic paste, and sauté for half a minute.

5. Lower the heat, add three tablespoons of *chole masala* and continue to sauté for another minute. Add the tomato purée and cook for three to four minutes.

6. Add the chickpeas along with the reserved stock and simmer for three to four minutes till the ghee rises to the surface. Sprinkle the remaining *chole masala* and chopped coriander, stir and cover immediately. Keep the *chole* warm.

7. Fill the *chole* in each of the fried *katori*. Drizzle one tablespoon of yogurt and top with the tamarind chutney and green chutney. Sprinkle the *sev* and chopped coriander, and serve immediately.

28
tiranga paneer tikka

These piquant morsels bursting with flavour are irresistible. No one can eat just one!

ingredients:

●450 grams cottage cheese ●½ teaspoon red chilli powder ●Salt to taste ●4 tablespoons Green Chutney (page 158) ●1 cup yogurt ●2 tablespoons gram flour ●½ tablespoon ginger paste ●½ tablespoon garlic paste ●4 tablespoons chopped fresh coriander ●4 green chillies, chopped ●1½ tablespoons lemon juice ●Melted butter for basting

method:

1. Grate one hundred grams of cottage cheese and cut the remaining into one-and-a-half-inch cubes. Slice each cube into two layers without cutting through.

2. In a bowl, mix together the grated cottage cheese, chilli powder and salt.

3. Take a cottage cheese cube, spread green chutney over the first layer, and cottage cheese mixture on the second layer.

4. In a deep bowl, mix together the yogurt, gram flour, ginger paste, garlic paste, chopped coriander, green chillies, salt and lemon juice. Add the stuffed cottage cheese cubes and mix gently so that all the cubes are evenly coated with the mixture. Set aside for about an hour.

5. Thread the cottage cheese cubes a little apart onto skewers and roast over a moderately hot charcoal grill for five to six minutes, basting them with melted butter once in between. You can also cook them on a hot non-stick *tawa* or griddle.

6. Serve immediately.

29
baby corn satay

There is something addictive about peanuts. Crushed into a thick sauce and served with barbecued baby corn, the addiction can only get stronger!

ingredients:

• 12 pieces of baby corn, blanched • 2 tablespoons oil • 1 medium onion, quartered, layers separated • 1 medium cucumber, cut into 1-inch cubes • 12 satay sticks

Marinade
• Salt to taste • 1 tablespoon soy sauce • 1 teaspoon lemon juice • 1 teaspoon garlic paste • 1 teaspoon ginger paste • 1 teaspoon brown sugar • ½ teaspoon honey

Peanut Sauce
• 6 tablespoons peanut paste • 1 tablespoon oil • 1 small onion, chopped • ½ inch ginger, chopped • 4 garlic cloves, chopped • ½ tablespoon soy sauce • 4 tablespoons Coconut Milk (page 159) • 1 tablespoon lemon juice • Salt to taste • 1 tablespoon honey • 1 fresh red chilli, seeded and chopped

method:

1. Place the baby corn in a bowl. Add the salt, soy sauce, lemon juice and mix well. Add the garlic and ginger pastes, brown sugar and honey, and mix again. Set aside to marinate for fifteen minutes.

2. Heat the oil on a non-stick griddle plate. Thread the marinated pieces of baby corn onto the satay sticks and place on the griddle plate. Pour some of the excess marinade over the baby corn. Turn the satay sticks on the griddle to cook the baby corn evenly.

3. For the peanut sauce, heat the oil in a non-stick pan; add the onion and sauté. Add the ginger and garlic, and continue to sauté. Add the soy sauce, peanut paste and four tablespoons of water. Stir and add the coconut milk, lemon juice, salt and honey.

4. Add the fresh red chilli and stir. Take the pan off the heat.

5. Thread the onion and cucumber pieces onto separate satay sticks.

6. Serve the baby corn and vegetable satay with the sauce.

30
vegetable tempura

Elegant, crisp and light – a delightful alternative to the usual *pakore* and *bhajia*, and one which I can never get enough of.

ingredients:

● 8 medium cauliflower florets ● 1 medium green capsicum, cut into 1-inch triangles ● 1 medium red capsicum, cut into 1-inch triangles ● 1 medium yellow capsicum, cut into 1-inch triangles ● 1 medium carrot, cut into thin round slices ● 1 medium onion, cut into 1-inch cubes and layers separated ● ½ teaspoon white pepper powder ● Salt to taste ● ¾ cup refined flour ● ½ cup cornflour ● ¼ teaspoon baking powder ● ¾ cup oil + for deep-frying

method:

1. Place all the vegetables in a bowl. Add the white pepper powder and salt, and toss well. Chill in the refrigerator for about fifteen minutes.

2. Mix the refined flour, cornflour, baking powder, three-fourth cup oil, salt to taste and three-fourth cup of chilled water. Whisk thoroughly to make a batter of pouring consistency. Set aside for twenty minutes.

3. Heat sufficient oil in a non-stick wok. Dip the vegetables, one by one, in the batter and deep-fry over medium heat, turning frequently, until crisp and golden brown. Drain on absorbent paper.

4. Serve hot with a sauce of your choice.

chef's tip:

For a crisper result, increase the quantity of oil in the batter. Whisk well to incorporate the oil thoroughly.

31
spicy moroccan wraps

Every time I eat this wrap, redolent with harissa, I think of the smells, the sounds, the hustle and bustle of the souks of Marrakesh.

ingredients:

● 4 cornmeal or wholewheat tortillas ● 1 large green zucchini, cut into ½-inch cubes ● 2 medium yellow capsicums, cut into ½-inch cubes ● 2 tablespoons olive oil ● ¼ teaspoon red chilli flakes ● Salt to taste ● ¼ teaspoon black pepper powder ● ¼ teaspoon mixed dried herbs ● 10-12 chopped green or black olives ● ½ cup sun-dried tomatoes, soaked in water and chopped ● 1 tablespoon chopped fresh parsley

Harrisa Sauce
● 6 dried red chillies ● 1 teaspoon coriander seeds ● 1 teaspoon caraway seeds ● 1 teaspoon cumin seeds ● 1 garlic clove, minced ● 1 tablespoon vinegar ● Salt to taste

method:

1. To make the harrisa sauce, soak the red chillies in one cup of water for ten minutes.

2. Dry-roast the coriander seeds, caraway seeds and cumin seeds till fragrant and grind them with the red chillies to a smooth paste. Transfer the mixture to a bowl, add the garlic, vinegar and salt, and mix well.

3. Preheat an oven to 180C/350F/Gas Mark 4.

4. Marinate the zucchini and yellow capsicums in a mixture of olive oil, chilli flakes, salt, pepper powder and mixed herbs for ten minutes.

5. Spread the vegetables out on a baking tray and roast them in the oven for twenty minutes.

6. Add the olives, sun-dried tomatoes and parsley to the roasted vegetables and mix. Stir in the harrisa sauce.

7. Spread the mixture over the tortillas and roll up firmly.

8. Serve immediately.

32

golden bags

Some would refer to them as *'potli'*, but that would not begin to describe these small crisp pouches of perfection.

ingredients:

●30 five-inch round spring roll wrappers ●1 cup crumbled cottage cheese ●½ cup minced mixed vegetables (cauliflower, French beans and green peas) ●1 tablespoon chopped fresh coriander ●¼ teaspoon black pepper powder ●Salt to taste ●2 tablespoons oil + for deep-frying ●10 garlic cloves, chopped ●A few spring onion greens ●½ cup sweet chilli sauce

method:

1. To make the filling, mix together the cottage cheese, vegetables, chopped coriander, pepper powder and salt.

2. Heat two tablespoons of oil in a non-stick wok; add the garlic and sauté until fragrant. Add the cottage cheese mixture and stir-fry for three to four minutes.

3. Place one tablespoon of the filling in the centre of each spring roll wrapper, and gather the edges together in pleats to make a bag (*potli*). Tie the bag tightly around the filling with a strip of spring onion green stalk. Trim the excess wrapper and spring onion.

4. Heat plenty of oil in a deep non-stick wok and deep-fry the bags until golden. Drain on absorbent paper.

5. Serve hot with sweet chilli sauce.

33

dhaniya adrak champe

I can rarely stop myself from taking a bite out of one of these succulent chops as soon as they emerge hissing and sizzling from the grill.

ingredients:

- 500 grams lamb chops

Marinade
- ½ small bunch (25 grams) fresh coriander, chopped • 2 inches ginger • 2 tablespoons chopped unripe papaya
- ½ teaspoon soda bicarbonate • 10 fresh spinach leaves • 4 green chillies • ½ cup drained (hung) yogurt
- 1 tablespoon vinegar • 1½ inches ginger, finely grated • 5-6 black peppercorns, crushed • 2 tablespoons roasted gram flour • Salt to taste • 1 tablespoon oil • 4 tablespoons melted butter

To Serve
- Mint Chutney (page 158)

method:

1. Pat the lamb chops dry with a kitchen towel. Flatten them with a rolling pin or with the back of a knife. Prick all over with a fork.

2. Grind the chopped coriander, ginger, papaya, soda bicarbonate, spinach and green chillies to a fine paste.

3. Place the ground paste in a bowl; add the yogurt, vinegar, grated ginger, crushed peppercorns, roasted gram flour, salt and oil, and mix well. Add the mutton chops, mix well and set aside in a refrigerator to marinate overnight.

4. Preheat an oven to 180C/350F/Gas Mark 4 or heat a gas *tandoor* over a medium heat.

5. Place the marinated chops on a greased wire rack or grill, and cover them with the marinade left in the bowl.

6. Grill the chops for twenty minutes, turning once in between. Baste with butter and grill for another fifteen minutes or till tender.

7. Serve with mint chutney.

34
mutton shammi kababs

These hearty cushions of pulverised meat may have had their origins in the Middle East, but we have made them our own. I particularly enjoy the symphony of textures and flavours in each bite – smooth, spicy kabab, crunchy, astringent onion rings and tangy mint chutney.

ingredients:

● 250 grams minced mutton ● 8 teaspoons oil + for deep-frying ● 1½ medium onions, chopped ● 2 tablespoons pure ghee ● ½ teaspoon caraway seeds ● 2 dried red chillies, broken ● ½ inch ginger, roughly chopped ● 5 garlic cloves, roughly chopped ● 1 tablespoons split Bengal gram, soaked for ½ hour ● 5 tablespoon chopped fresh mint ● 5 tablespoons chopped fresh coriander ● ½ tablespoon lemon juice ● Salt to taste ● 1 egg, beaten

To Serve
● Mint Chutney (page 158)

method:

1. Heat sufficient oil in a non-stick *kadai* and deep-fry the onions till brown. Drain on absorbent paper.

2. Heat the ghee in a non-stick pan; add the caraway seeds, red chillies, ginger and garlic, and sauté for one minute.

3. Add the minced mutton and sauté for five minutes, stirring occasionally.

4. Drain the split Bengal gram and add to the pan. Stir and sauté for one minute.

5. Add the chopped mint and chopped coriander, and stir well. Cook for five minutes and set aside to cool.

6. Grind the mixture together with the fried onions, lemon juice and salt, to a coarse paste. Divide the paste into eight equal portions and shape into round patties and flatten slightly.

7. Heat two teaspoons oil in a shallow non-stick pan. Dip two kababs in the beaten egg and shallow-fry for three or four minutes till golden brown on both sides.

8. Serve hot with mint chutney and onion rings.

35
salt and pepper prawns

A flaming hot wok and some swashbuckling stir-frying will keep these prawns crisp and juicy at the same time.

ingredients:

● 300 grams king prawns ● Salt to taste ● ½ teaspoon black pepper powder ● 4 black peppercorns, crushed ● 2 tablespoons cornflour ● 2 tablespoons light soy sauce ● 1½ tablespoons oil + for deep-frying ● 3 garlic cloves, crushed ● ¾ inch ginger, chopped ● 2 spring onions, sliced ● 3 spring onion green stalks, sliced

method:

1. Peel the prawns leaving the tails intact; devein and wash thoroughly.

2. In a bowl, combine the salt, one-fourth teaspoon pepper powder, half the crushed peppercorns, one tablespoon of cornflour and one tablespoon of soy sauce. Add the prawns, mix well and set aside to marinate for fifteen minutes.

3. Mix the remaining cornflour with two tablespoons of water.

4. Heat sufficient oil in a non-stick wok and deep-fry the prawns for two minutes. Drain on absorbent paper.

5. In a separate non-stick wok, heat one and a half tablespoons of oil; add the garlic, ginger and spring onions, and sauté for two minutes on high heat.

6. Add the prawns, salt, remaining pepper powder, half the remaining crushed peppercorns, remaining soy sauce, the cornflour mixture and spring onion greens. Stir-fry on high heat for four minutes, or until the prawns are cooked through.

7. Sprinkle the remaining crushed peppercorns and serve hot.

36

chao tom
(prawn on
a sugarcane stick)

I cannot resist chewing on the edible skewers after feasting on the succulent prawn kababs.

ingredients:

● 8 six-inch sugarcane sticks, peeled ● 2 tablespoons oil for greasing

Seasoned Prawns
● 300 grams medium prawns, peeled and deveined ● 1 teaspoon salt ● ¼ cup minced chicken ● ¼ cup flaked white fish fillet ● 3 garlic cloves ● 3 shallots ● 1 teaspoon sugar ● 1 egg white, beaten ● 1 tablespoon fish sauce ● 1 tablespoon roasted rice powder ● ¼ teaspoon black pepper powder

To Garnish
● 1 head iceberg lettuce, leaves separated ● 80 grams rice vermicelli (optional), blanched and drained ● 4 shallots, sliced and crisply fried ● A few sprigs of fresh coriander ● A few sprigs of fresh mint

To Serve
● Fish Sauce Dip (see below)

method:

1. Rub salt into the prawns and set aside for fifteen minutes. Rinse and drain.

2. Grind together the prawns, chicken, fish, garlic, shallots and sugar to a paste in a blender. Add the egg white, fish sauce, roasted rice powder and pepper powder, and mix well. Divide into eight equal portions.

3. Lightly grease your hands, wrap a portion of the prawn mixture tightly around the middle of a sugarcane stick. Repeat this with the remaining mixture and sugarcane sticks.

4. Heat a non-stick grill pan and grill the sticks over medium heat for five to ten minutes, rotating them frequently, until lightly browned on all sides. Remove and place on a plate.

5. On individual serving plates, arrange the lettuce leaves, rice vermicelli, fried shallots, coriander and mint. Arrange the prawn sticks on top and serve with the fish sauce dip.

Fish Sauce Dip
Grind together coarsely, 2-3 seeded and sliced fresh red chillies and 2 garlic cloves. Add ¼ cup sugar, 3 tablespoons lemon juice, 1 tablespoon vinegar, 3 tablespoons fish sauce, salt to taste and stir until the sugar dissolves and set aside.

37

kadai prawns with roasted pepper jam

Kipling could not have been more wrong – east and west do meet and mingle successfully in this dish of plump prawns and sticky, spicy jam.

ingredients:

●400 grams large prawns, peeled and deveined ●4 dried red chillies, broken into bits ●1 teaspoon coriander seeds ●2 tablespoons lemon juice ●Salt to taste ●1½ tablespoons oil ●1 teaspoon carom seeds ●1 medium onion, chopped ●1 teaspoon ginger-garlic paste ●2 green chillies, chopped ●½ teaspoon roasted and crushed dried fenugreek leaves ●¾ cup Roasted Pepper Jam (see below) ●2 tablespoons chopped fresh coriander ●½ teaspoon *garam masala* powder

Roasted Pepper Jam

●4 medium red capsicums, quartered ●2 medium tomatoes, seeded and quartered ●Salt to taste ●1 teaspoon oil ●3-4 garlic cloves, chopped ●3 tablespoons cider vinegar ●2 tablespoons brown sugar ●2 teaspoons red chilli flakes

method:

1. Preheat an oven to 180C/350F/Gas Mark 4.

2. To make the roasted pepper jam, arrange the capsicums and tomatoes on a baking tray. Sprinkle with salt. Bake in the preheated oven for twenty to twenty-five minutes and set aside to cool. When completely cold, peel the capsicums and tomatoes and purée them in a blender.

3. Heat the oil in a non-stick pan; add the garlic and sauté for thirty seconds. Add the capsicum-tomato purée and cook for two minutes. Stir in the vinegar and bring to a boil. Simmer and add the brown sugar, chilli flakes and salt. Cook till reduced to half the quantity. Remove from the heat and set aside.

4. Dry-roast the red chillies and coriander seeds. Cool and grind coarsely.

5. Marinate the prawns in the ground *masala*, lemon juice and salt for fifteen minutes.

6. Heat the oil in a non-stick pan; add the carom seeds. When they begin to splutter, add the onion and sauté till golden brown. Add the ginger-garlic paste and green chillies, and sauté for thirty seconds.

7. Add the marinated prawns and stir-fry for a few minutes. Add one-fourth cup of water and cook till tender. Add the dried fenugreek leaves and mix well.

8. Add the roasted pepper jam and mix till all the prawns are coated well with the jam.

9. Garnish with chopped coriander and *garam masala* powder, and serve hot.

38

fish cakes with cucumber relish

Watch the sparks fly as sizzling fish meets cool cucumber. I find the combination irresistible.

ingredients:

• 4 (300 grams) white fish fillets, cut into chunks • Salt to taste • 2 tablespoons Red Curry Paste (page 159) • 1 egg • 1 tablespoon fish sauce • 1 teaspoon sugar • 3 tablespoons cornflour • 1 tablespoon chopped fresh coriander • 10-12 French beans, chopped and blanched • 3 tablespoons breadcrumbs + to coat • Oil for deep-frying

Cucumber Relish
• 1 medium cucumber, quartered and sliced • 4 tablespoons rice vinegar • 1 tablespoon sugar • 2 garlic cloves, chopped • 4 shallots, sliced • 1½ inches ginger, chopped

method:

1. To make the cucumber relish, boil together the rice vinegar, two tablespoons water and the sugar in a non-stick pan. Stir until the sugar dissolves, remove from the heat and cool.

2. Mix the cucumber, garlic, shallots and ginger in a bowl and pour the vinegar mixture over it.

3. Boil the fish in salted water, drain thoroughly and cool.

4. Place the red curry paste, fish and egg in a food processor and blend well. Transfer the mixture to a bowl. Add the fish sauce, sugar, cornflour, chopped coriander, French beans and three tablespoons of breadcrumbs, and mix well.

5. Shape the mixture into cakes (patties) about two inches in diameter and a quarter inch thick. Roll in breadcrumbs.

6. Heat plenty of oil in a non-stick wok and deep-fry the fish cakes, a few at a time, for four to five minutes. Drain on absorbent paper.

7. Serve hot with the cucumber relish.

39
chettinad kozhi varuval (chettinad fried chicken)

Tamil's great gift to the culinary lexicon is the word *'kari'*. The aroma of fried curry leaves is what gives this dish its characteristic flavour.

ingredients:

●1 whole (800 grams) chicken ●2 medium onions, roughly chopped ●1 inch ginger, roughly chopped ●5 garlic cloves, roughly chopped ●4 green chillies, roughly chopped ●6 dried red chillies, broken into 2 pieces ●½ teaspoon turmeric powder ●1 tablespoon lemon juice ●2 tablespoons rice flour ●Salt to taste ●15 curry leaves, finely shredded ●1 cup oil

method:

1. Split the chicken through the backbone and the breast, into two equal halves. Make three or four half-inch deep cuts on the breast and leg pieces.

2. Grind the onions, ginger, garlic, green chillies and red chillies with three tablespoons of water to a smooth paste.

3. Mix the turmeric powder, lemon juice, rice flour and salt into the *masala* paste.

4. Coat the chicken liberally with the paste; add the curry leaves and mix. Cover the bowl with cling film and leave to marinate for two or three hours in a refrigerator. Remove the bowl from the refrigerator and remove the chicken pieces from the marinade. Reserve the marinade.

5. Heat the oil in a non-stick *kadai*; add the marinated chicken and sauté over high heat for two minutes on both sides to seal the juices.

6. Lower the heat to medium, cover with a lid and cook for fifteen to twenty minutes, turning over and basting frequently with the remaining marinade. Sprinkle two or three tablespoons of water if the chicken starts drying out.

7. When the chicken is cooked, continue to cook over high heat for six to seven minutes longer, so that the surface of the chicken is crisp and golden brown.

8. Cut into smaller pieces and serve hot.

40
yakitori chicken with spring onions

Japan on a stick is how I think of these tender barbecued chicken cubes coated with a Japanese sake and soy sauce.

ingredients:

● 500 grams boneless chicken thigh or breast pieces, cut into 1-inch cubes ● 4 spring onions, halved
● 1 large red capsicum, cut into 1-inch pieces ● 4 button mushrooms, halved ● 8 fresh shiitake mushrooms
● 2 tablespoons oil ● 8 satay sticks

Sauce
● ½ cup sake ● ½ cup Japanese soy sauce ● 2 tablespoons sugar ● Salt to taste ● ½ teaspoon black pepper powder

method:

1. To make the sauce, pour the sake into a small non-stick pan; add the soy sauce and sugar, and bring the mixture to a boil. Add the salt and pepper powder, and mix. Lower the heat and simmer, uncovered, over medium heat until the sauce reduces to one-third. Remove from the heat and set aside to cool.

2. Thread onto each satay stick a spring onion half, two chicken cubes, a piece of red capsicum, half a button mushroom, a shiitake mushroom, two more chicken cubes and finally a piece of red capsicum. Leave a little space between each ingredient to allow even cooking.

3. Heat one tablespoon of oil on a non-stick *tawa*. Place four satay sticks at a time on it and cook, turning and brushing with the sauce occasionally, until browned all over and cooked through.

4. Serve the yakitori sprinkled with remaining sauce.

|main courses|

41
baghare baingan

This is one of those rich, iconic *Nizami* dishes that I am always happy to indulge in. The humble brinjal, steeped in an aromatic nutty gravy, is transformed into an Indian gourmet delight.

ingredients:

●250 grams small brinjals ●2 medium onions, quartered ●1½ teaspoons coriander seeds ●1½ tablespoons sesame seeds ●2 tablespoons peanuts ●½ teaspoon cumin seeds ●¾ teaspoon poppy seeds ●1 tablespoon grated dried coconut ●A pinch of fenugreek seeds ●1 inch ginger, chopped ●6-8 garlic cloves, chopped ●Salt to taste ●A pinch of turmeric powder ●½ teaspoon red chilli powder ●½ teaspoon grated jaggery or sugar ●2 tablespoons Tamarind Pulp (page 158) ●4 tablespoons oil ●A sprig of curry leaves

method:

1. Wash the brinjals and slit lengthways into four, with the quarters held together at the stalk end.

2. Dry-roast the onions on a non-stick *tawa* till soft and pale gold. Dry-roast the coriander seeds, sesame seeds, peanuts, cumin seeds, poppy seeds, dried coconut and fenugreek seeds all together till fragrant and they begin to change colour.

3. Grind together the roasted onions, roasted spices, ginger, garlic, salt, turmeric powder, chilli powder and jaggery to a very fine paste. Add the tamarind pulp and mix well. Stuff the slit brinjals with some *masala* and reserve the rest.

4. Heat the oil in a non-stick *kadai*; add the curry leaves and sauté for one minute. Add the stuffed brinjals and sauté for about ten minutes. Add the reserved *masala* and mix gently. Add two cups of water, cover and cook over low heat till the brinjals are completely cooked and the oil rises to the surface. Serve hot.

42

dahiwale amrud

The inclusion of ripe fruit in spicy curries has always fascinated me. The *jugalbandi* of sweet and savoury flavours on the tongue is sheer bliss.

ingredients:

● ½ cup yogurt ● 4 medium guavas, seeded and cut into small pieces ● ½ tablespoon coriander powder ● ¼ teaspoon red chilli powder ● ¼ teaspoon turmeric powder ● 1 teaspoon dried mango powder ● 1 tablespoon ghee ● 2 green chillies, chopped ● ½ teaspoon cumin seeds ● ½ teaspoon fennel seeds ● ¼ teaspoon asafoetida ● 1 medium tomato, chopped ● Salt to taste ● ¼ teaspoon *garam masala* powder ● ½ teaspoon sugar

method:

1. Whisk the yogurt with all the powdered spices, except the *garam masala* powder.

2. Heat the ghee in a non-stick *kadai*; add the green chillies, cumin seeds, fennel seeds and asafoetida, and stir to mix.

3. Add the whisked yogurt, tomato and salt, and stir for a few seconds.

4. Add three-fourth cup of water and bring to a boil. Add the guavas and let the gravy come to a boil again. Lower the heat, cover and cook, stirring occasionally, till the guavas are cooked.

5. Add the *garam masala* powder and cook for another three or four minutes.

6. Sprinkle the sugar and stir. Serve hot.

43

dahi papad ki sabzi

Papad lurking at the back of your kitchen cabinet can be elevated from its status as an accompaniment to that of a prime ingredient in this flavourful yogurt-based gravy!

ingredients:

- 1½ cups sour yogurt • 4 Bikaneri *moong papad* • ¾ tablespoon gram flour • ½ teaspoon turmeric powder
- ¾ teaspoon red chilli powder • Salt to taste • 1½ tablespoons pure ghee • 1 teaspoon cumin seeds
- 1½ teaspoons coriander powder • ½ teaspoon asafoetida • 2 dried red chillies, broken into bits • ¼ cup *boondi*
- 1 tablespoon chopped fresh coriander • ½ teaspoon *garam masala* powder

method:

1. In a large bowl, combine the yogurt, gram flour, turmeric powder, chilli powder and salt. Add two cups of water and whisk till smooth. Strain and set aside.

2. Heat the ghee in a non-stick *kadai*; add the cumin seeds. When they change colour, add the coriander powder and sauté for one minute.

3. Add the asafoetida and red chillies, and sauté for half a minute.

4. Add the yogurt mixture and adjust the seasoning. Stir continuously till the mixture comes to a boil. Lower the heat and simmer for two minutes.

5. Heat a non-stick *tawa* and roast the *papad* on both sides. Roughly break each one into two-inch pieces.

6. Add the papad and *boondi* to the simmering yogurt mixture. Boil for two to three minutes.

7. Garnish with chopped coriander and *garam masala* powder. Serve hot.

44
aviyal

The subtle interplay between the delicately spiced coconut gravy and the cornucopia of rustic vegetables is what makes Aviyal one of my favourite South Indian dishes.

ingredients:

●1 medium carrot ●6-8 French beans ●6-8 broad beans ●200 grams white pumpkin ●1 medium unripe banana ●1 drumstick ●100 grams yam ●¼ cup shelled green peas ●Salt to taste ●½ cup grated fresh coconut ●4 green chillies ●1½ teaspoons cumin seeds ●1 tablespoon rice ●1½ cups yogurt ●10-12 curry leaves ●2 tablespoons coconut oil

method:

1. Cut the carrot, French beans, broad beans, pumpkin, banana, drumstick and yam into thick fingers not more than two-inches long.

2. Boil the yam separately in salted water, drain and reserve.

3. Grind the coconut, green chillies, cumin seeds and rice with a little water to a fine paste. Whisk the yogurt with the ground paste and set aside.

4. Cook the rest of the vegetables in one and half cups of water with salt and the curry leaves till almost tender.

5. Add the yogurt mixture and yam, and stir thoroughly. Bring to simmering point and remove from heat.

6. Stir in the coconut oil and serve hot.

45

achaari gobhi

This dish takes me back to an aunt's home in Amritsar, where cauliflower picked from the vegetable patch was cooked with pickling spices and yogurt, and eaten with hot *roti* straight off the *tawa*.

ingredients:

● 1 medium cauliflower ● 1½ tablespoons mustard oil ● ½ teaspoon mustard seeds ● ½ teaspoon cumin seeds ● ¼ teaspoon fenugreek seeds ● ½ teaspoon fennel seeds ● ¼ teaspoon onion seeds ● 1 teaspoon coriander seeds, crushed ● ¼ teaspoon asafoetida ● 1 medium onion, chopped ● 1 teaspoon ginger paste ● 1 teaspoon garlic paste ● 3 green chillies, chopped ● Salt to taste ● ½ teaspoon turmeric powder ● ¾ cup yogurt

method:

1. Separate the cauliflower into large florets.

2. Heat the mustard oil to smoking point in a non stick *kadai*; add the mustard seeds, cumin seeds, fenugreek seeds, fennel seeds, onion seeds, crushed coriander seeds and asafoetida, and sauté till they begin to change colour.

3. Add the onion and sauté till translucent. Add the ginger paste, garlic paste and green chillies, and sauté till the onions turn light brown.

4. Add the cauliflower and salt, and sauté over medium heat till brown.

5. Add the turmeric powder and one cup of water, and cook, covered, for ten to fifteen minutes, or till the cauliflower is tender.

6. Add the yogurt and continue to cook till the water evaporates and the gravy coats the cauliflower.

7. Serve hot.

46
capsicum kayras

Konkan food has a special place in my heart. A bowl of this sweet and sour dish with the keynote flavours of the Konkan - coconut, tamarind and jaggery - accompanied by a few thin *roti* is one of my favourite meals.

ingredients:

- 5-6 medium green capsicums, cut into 1-inch pieces • 2 medium potatoes, cut into 1-inch cubes • ½ cup peanuts • 1 tablespoon oil • ½ teaspoon mustard seeds • A pinch of asafoetida • ¼ teaspoon turmeric powder • Salt to taste • 1½ tablespoons grated jaggery

Masala
- ½ cup grated coconut • 3 tablespoons sesame seeds • ½ tablespoon oil • 2 tablespoons split Bengal gram • 2 tablespoons coriander seeds • ¼ teaspoon fenugreek seeds • 4-5 dried red chillies • 2 tablespoons Tamarind Pulp (page 158)

method:

1. For the *masala*, separately dry-roast the coconut and sesame seeds in a non-stick pan till fragrant and lightly coloured. Transfer to a plate and set aside to cool.

2. Heat half a tablespoon of oil in the same pan; add the split Bengal gram, coriander seeds, fenugreek seeds and red chillies, and sauté till fragrant. Grind along with the roasted coconut and sesame seeds, and the tamarind pulp to a fine paste with three-fourth cup of water.

3. Heat the oil in a non-stick pan; add the mustard seeds and when they begin to splutter, add the asafoetida. Add the peanuts and sauté for three to four minutes.

4. Add the potatoes, turmeric powder, salt and jaggery. Stir, cover and cook over low heat for five minutes. Add the capsicum, stir and cook till the vegetables are partially cooked.

5. Add the ground paste and one and a half cups of water, and cook over low heat for three to four minutes. Serve hot.

47

chole dhania masala

Much as I love the traditional Punjabi *chole*, this dish has a slight edge as it incorporates the flavour of fresh coriander which is my favourite herb.

ingredients:

• ¾ cup chickpeas • 1½ teaspoons coriander seeds • 50 grams fresh coriander • ¼ cup split Bengal gram • Salt to taste • ½ inch cinnamon • 1½ teaspoons cumin seeds • 1 black cardamom • 4-5 cloves • 2 green chillies • 2 tablespoons ghee • 1 medium onion, sliced • 1 teaspoon garlic paste • 1 teaspoon ginger paste • ½ tablespoon dried mango powder • ½ teaspoon *garam masala* powder • Black salt to taste • ¼ teaspoon red chilli powder

method:

1. Soak the chickpeas and split Bengal gram separately for four to six hours. Drain, mix, add three cups of water and a little salt, and pressure-cook till the pressure is released five to six times (five to six whistles).

2. Lightly roast and powder the cinnamon, cumin seeds, coriander seeds, black cardamom and cloves. Grind together the fresh coriander and green chillies to a smooth paste.

3. Heat one and a half tablespoons ghee in a non-stick *kadai*; add the onion and sauté for three to four minutes till golden brown. Add the garlic paste and ginger paste, and continue to sauté for another minute.

4. Add the spice powder, dried mango powder, *garam masala* powder, black salt and coriander paste, and sauté for two to three minutes or till the ghee separates from the *masala*.

5. Add the chickpeas and split Bengal gram, and mix. Add half a cup of water if the mixture is too dry. Adjust the salt and let the mixture come to a boil. Lower the heat and simmer for four to five minutes.

6. Heat the remaining ghee in a small non-stick pan; take it off the heat and add the chilli powder and immediately pour over the *chana*. Cover immediately and leave to stand for five minutes.

7. Serve hot with *roti* or *puri*.

48

shaam savera

Shaam Savera has come to be known as my signature dish. It is one of my earliest creations and an impromptu take on the *palak kofta* that I was scheduled to present on TV.

ingredients:

Kofte

●1.2 kilograms spinach ●65 grams cottage cheese, grated ●2 tablespoons oil + for deep-frying ●1 teaspoon cumin seeds ●10-12 garlic cloves, finely chopped ●6-7 green chillies, finely chopped ●Salt to taste ●¼ teaspoon turmeric powder ●4 tablespoons gram flour ●A pinch of green cardamom powder ●¼ cup cornflour

Makhni Gravy

●1 cup butter ●2 tablespoons oil ●12 green cardamoms ●½ blade of mace ●20 garlic cloves, roughly chopped with the skin ●2½ teaspoons *deggi mirch* powder ●18 large tomatoes, roughly chopped ●Salt to taste ●2 teaspoons dried fenugreek leaves, roasted and powdered ●3 tablespoons honey ●8 tablespoons fresh cream

method:

1. For the *kofte*, blanch the spinach in eight cups of boiling water for two to three minutes. Drain and refresh in cold water. Squeeze out the water, cool and chop finely. Heat two tablespoons of oil in a non-stick pan; add the cumin seeds, garlic and green chillies, and sauté for a few seconds. Add the salt and turmeric powder, and stir. Add the gram flour and continue to sauté for one or two minutes. Add the spinach and sauté, stirring continuously, until the mixture is dry and begins to leave the sides of the pan. Set aside to cool. Divide into eight equal portions.

2. In a bowl, mash the cottage cheese with a little salt and a pinch of green cardamom powder. Divide into eight equal portions and roll into balls. Take each spinach portion, flatten it on your palm and place the cottage cheese ball in the centre. Gather the edges and shape into a ball. Spread the cornflour on a plate and roll the stuffed spinach balls in it, shaking off the excess cornflour. Heat sufficient oil in a non-stick *kadai*. Fry one *kofta*, if it breaks, add more sautéed gram flour. Deep-fry the *kofte* sliding them into the oil gently on low heat, for two to three minutes till golden brown. Drain on absorbent paper.

3. For the *makhni* gravy, heat the oil in a deep non-stick pan. Add the cardamoms and mace, and sauté till fragrant. Add the garlic and sauté for one minute. Mix the chilli powder in three tablespoons water to make a paste. Add this paste to the pan and continue to sauté for thirty seconds. Add the tomatoes and salt, and cook for fifteen minutes, or till the tomatoes turn pulpy. Strain the tomato mixture into another deep non-stick pan. Grind the residue to a smooth paste. Strain, and add the paste to the pan. Add three-fourth cup of water and stir well.

4. Place the pan on a heated non-stick *tawa*. Add the butter and simmer, stirring occasionally, for ten minutes or till the raw flavour of the tomatoes disappears. Stir in the dried fenugreek leaves and honey, and cook for five minutes longer. Stir in the fresh cream and cook for two minutes. To serve, cut the *kofte* in half and arrange in a pool of *makhni* gravy.

49
ekadashi jeera aloo

Cumin and potatoes have a symbiotic relationship. Every cuisine has a dish of potatoes spiced with cumin, which is one of the most ancient spices known to man. This 'fasting food' is a particular favourite and represents my love for Mumbai and Maharashtrian food.

ingredients:

500 grams baby potatoes, parboiled and halved ● 1 teaspoon cumin seeds ● 2 tablespoons oil ● 15-18 curry leaves ● 2 green chillies, slit ● Rock salt to taste ● 1½ teaspoons sugar ● 2 tablespoons lemon juice ● 2 tablespoons chopped fresh coriander ● 1½ tablespoons grated coconut

method:

1. Heat the oil in a non-stick *kadai*; add the cumin seeds, curry leaves and green chillies, and sauté till they begin to change colour.

2. Add the potatoes and rock salt, and sauté over medium heat for two minutes. Cover and cook over low heat till the potatoes are completely done and well browned.

3. Add the sugar, lemon juice, chopped coriander and coconut. Toss well to mix.

4. Serve hot.

50

bhare
baghare
tamatar

Fine dining *Nizami*-style – ripe, red tomatoes filled with a creamy cheese filling, nestled in a rich gravy – *wah*!

ingredients:

• 8 medium firm red tomatoes • 1½ tablespoons unsalted butter • 5-6 medium fresh button mushrooms, chopped • ½ cup grated cottage cheese • 3 tablespoons grated processed cheese • ½ medium red capsicum, chopped • 2 teaspoons chopped fresh coriander • 2 green chillies, chopped • 12 cashew nuts, halved • Salt to taste • ¾ cup raw shelled peanuts • 1 tablespoon oil + for deep-frying • 2 medium onions, sliced • ¼ teaspoon mustard seeds • ¼ teaspoon cumin seeds • ½ teaspoon caraway seeds • 8 curry leaves • 1½ tablespoons ginger paste • 1 tablespoons garlic paste • ¼ cup Tamarind Pulp (page 158) • 1 teaspoon red chilli powder • ½ teaspoon turmeric powder • 2 teaspoons coriander powder • ½ teaspoon roasted cumin powder

method:

1. Blanch the tomatoes in boiling salted water for half a minute. Drain and peel. Slice off the top of each tomato and scoop out the seeds to make cups. Heat the butter in a non-stick pan and sauté the mushrooms until all the moisture evaporates. Remove and cool.

2. Mix together the mushrooms, cottage cheese, processed cheese, capsicum, chopped coriander, green chillies, cashew nuts and salt. Spoon the mixture into the tomato cups and set aside.

3. Roast the peanuts, cool and grind with a little water into a fine paste.

4. Heat sufficient oil in a non-stick *kadai* and deep-fry the onions till golden brown. Drain on absorbent paper.

5. Heat one tablespoon of oil in a separate non-stick *kadai*; add the mustard seeds, cumin seeds and caraway seeds, and sauté till they begin to splutter. Add the curry leaves and sauté for half a minute. Add the ginger paste and garlic paste, and sauté until lightly browned. Stir in the tamarind pulp and sauté for three or four minutes over medium heat.

6. Add the fried onions, chilli powder, turmeric powder, coriander powder and cumin powder, and continue to sauté till the oil rises to the surface. Add the peanut paste and sauté until the mixture thickens. Add three cups of water and salt, and bring to a boil. Lower the heat; carefully add the stuffed tomatoes to the simmering gravy, and cook for four or five minute. Do not overcook the tomatoes; they should be firm and hold their shape. Serve hot.

51
chicken teriyaki
with black grapes

This is my take on the Japanese classic. I have replaced the sake with white wine for a more mellow flavour. The molasses adds a rich sheen to the sauce and the black grapes a sweet and sour note.

ingredients:

● 4 (150 grams each) chicken breasts ● 4 tablespoons soy sauce ● 2 tablespoons molasses ● Salt to taste ● ½ teaspoon black pepper powder ● 2 tablespoons oil ● 1 cup bean sprouts ● Enoki mushrooms, to garnish

Sauce
● 12-15 black grapes, crushed ● 2 tablespoons butter ● 1 inch ginger, sliced ● 1 medium onion, finely chopped ● ½ cup white wine ● 1 tablespoon soy sauce ● ½ teaspoon black pepper powder ● Salt to taste ● 1 tablespoon molasses ● 2 tablespoons honey

method:

1. In a bowl, mix together the soy sauce, molasses, salt and pepper powder. Marinate the chicken breasts in this mixture for half an hour.

2. To make the sauce, heat the butter in a non-stick pan. Add the ginger and onion, and sauté till golden brown. Add the white wine and cook till the mixture reduces a little.

3. Add the crushed grapes and continue to cook, stirring continuously, for five to seven minutes till the grapes soften.

4. Stir in the soy sauce, pepper powder, salt and molasses. Mix well and strain the sauce.

5. Remove the chicken breasts from the marinade and place them on a preheated grill. Pour some of the marinade over the chicken and add the rest to the sauce.

6. Brush the chicken breasts with some oil and grill till done.

7. Pour the strained sauce into a non-stick pan and place on heat. Add the honey and reduce the sauce a little.

8. Arrange the bean sprouts on a serving plate. Place the chicken breasts on the sprouts. Pour the hot sauce over and serve with Enoki mushrooms.

chef's tip:

You can use honey if molasses is not available; in which case use dark soy sauce.

52

green chilli chicken

Tongue-blistering, as the quantity of chillies called for appears to be, you will be pleasantly surprised by the relative mildness of the dish, especially if you keep the small chillies whole.

ingredients:

●1 whole (800 grams) chicken, cut into 1½-inch pieces ●1 cup whole small green chillies ●3 green chillies, chopped ●2 medium onions, quartered ●10 garlic cloves ●1½ inches ginger, sliced ●½ cup chopped fresh coriander ●Salt to taste ●3 tablespoons oil ●¾ teaspoon cumin seeds ●¼ teaspoon turmeric powder ●1 teaspoon roasted cumin powder ●2 teaspoons coriander powder ●1 teaspoon *garam masala* powder

method:

1. Grind together the chopped green chillies, onions, garlic, ginger, chopped coriander and salt. Marinate the chicken in this mixture for about half an hour.

2. Heat the oil in a non-stick *kadai* and add the cumin seeds. When they begin to change colour, add the turmeric powder.

3. Add the marinated chicken and the whole small green chillies, and mix well. Add the cumin powder and coriander powder, and stir to mix.

4. Add the *garam masala* powder and adjust the seasoning. Stir in half a cup of water, cover and cook over medium heat for eight to ten minutes.

5. Lower the heat and cook for another eight to ten minutes, or till the chicken is tender. Serve hot.

53
butter chicken

How do I count the ways I love this dish! Always at the top of any Indian menu, I cannot resist its charms, no matter the range of exotica on offer.

ingredients:

● 2 tablespoons butter ● 400 grams skinned, boneless chicken, cut into 1½-inch pieces ● 1 teaspoon Kashmiri chilli powder ● 1 tablespoon lemon juice ● Salt to taste ● A few chopped fresh coriander leaves, to garnish ● A few finely cut ginger strips, to garnish

Marinade
● ½ cup yogurt ● 2 teaspoons ginger paste ● 2 teaspoons garlic paste ● ½ teaspoon Kashmiri chilli powder ● ½ teaspoon *garam masala* powder ● Salt to taste ● 2 teaspoons mustard oil

Makhni Gravy
● 2 tablespoons butter ● 2 green cardamoms ● 2 cloves ● 2-3 black peppercorns ● 1 inch cinnamon ● 1 teaspoon ginger paste ● 1 teaspoon garlic paste ● ½ cup tomato purée ● ½ teaspoon red chilli powder ● Salt to taste ● 2 tablespoons sugar or honey ● ½ teaspoon dried fenugreek leaves, powdered ● ½ cup fresh cream

method:

1. Rub a mixture of chilli powder, lemon juice and salt into the chicken and marinate for half an hour in the refrigerator.

2. For the marinade, tie the yogurt in a piece of muslin and hang over a bowl for fifteen to twenty minutes to drain. Transfer the thick yogurt to another bowl. Add the ginger and garlic pastes, chilli and *garam masala* powders, salt and mustard oil.

3. Add the marinade to the chicken and place in the refrigerator for three to four hours to marinate.

4. Preheat an oven to 200C/400F/Gas Mark 6.

5. Thread the chicken pieces onto skewers and cook in the preheated oven or a moderately hot *tandoor* for ten to twelve minutes, or until almost done. Baste with butter and cook for another two minutes. Remove and set aside.

6. To make the *makhni* gravy, heat the butter in a non-stick pan. Add the cardamoms, cloves, peppercorns and cinnamon, and sauté for two minutes. Add the ginger and garlic pastes, and sauté for two minutes.

7. Add the tomato purée, chilli powder, salt and half a cup of water, and bring the mixture to a boil. Lower the heat and simmer for ten minutes.

8. Stir in the sugar or honey and powdered dried fenugreek leaves. Add the cooked chicken and cook over low heat for five minutes. Stir in the fresh cream.

9. Garnish with the chopped coriander and ginger strips, and serve hot with *naan* or *parantha*.

54
patrani machchi (fish in banana leaves)

My Parsi friends never fail to serve me these delightful packages when I visit. Unwrapping the leaves to reveal their fragrant contents is an experience I look forward to with child-like anticipation.

ingredients:

- 8 (200 grams each) pomfret fillets • Salt to taste • 2 tablespoons lemon juice • 2 cups fresh coriander
- 5 green chillies • 1 cup grated coconut • 4 teaspoons cumin seeds • 12 garlic cloves • 2 teaspoons sugar
- 4 banana leaves

method:

1. Cut each fish fillet in half. Sprinkle a little salt and one tablespoon lemon juice, and set aside for half an hour, preferably in the refrigerator.

2. Grind the fresh coriander, green chillies, coconut, cumin seeds and garlic, with two to three tablespoons of water, to make a smooth chutney. Add the salt, sugar and remaining lemon juice, and mix well.

3. Spread the chutney on the fish fillets and leave to stand for at least fifteen minutes.

4. Cut the banana leaves into two pieces each. Pass the leaves over an open flame to make them soft and pliable.

5. Place two marinated pieces of fish in the centre of each banana leaf and fold in the ends of the leaf to enclose the fish completely.

6. Heat sufficient water in a steamer on high heat. Arrange the fish parcels on a steaming rack and place in the steamer. Lower the heat to medium, cover the steamer with the lid and steam for fifteen minutes.

7. Serve the fish in the leaf itself so that each guest can open the parcel and enjoy the fish hot.

chef's tip:

Traditionally this dish is steamed. But you can also cook the banana-wrapped fish on a non-stick pan, on medium heat, turning frequently so that the banana leaf does not burn.

55
malabar prawn curry

I have been trying for years to decide which my favourite prawn curry is. I am still not sure, but this Kerala version with green mangoes is certainly a contender.

ingredients:

- 500 grams small prawns • 1 teaspoon turmeric powder • Salt to taste • 1½ cups grated coconut
- 5 tablespoons oil • 10-12 shallots, halved • 1 tablespoon red chilli powder • 1 tablespoon coriander powder
- 2 green chillies, slit • 4 dried yogurt chillies • 10-12 curry leaves • 1 tablespoon Tamarind Pulp (page 158)
- 1 tablespoon coconut oil • 1 teaspoon fenugreek seeds, crushed lightly • 4 dried red chillies • 2 drumsticks, cut into pieces • 2 medium-sized unripe mangoes, peeled and cut into wedges

method:

1. Pat the prawns dry with a kitchen towel and place in a bowl. Add the turmeric powder and salt, and mix. Cover the bowl with cling film and place in a refrigerator to marinate for half an hour.

2. Soak the coconut in one cup of warm water for fifteen minutes. Grind to a fine paste.

3. Heat three tablespoons of oil in a non-stick deep pan; add the shallots and sauté till translucent. Add the chilli powder and coriander powder, slit green chillies, yogurt chillies, curry leaves and tamarind pulp, and sauté for one minute. Add the coconut paste and three cups of water, and cook till the curry reduces to half its quantity and thickens.

4. Strain the curry into a deep bowl, pressing down well to extract all the flavour. Set aside.

5. Heat the remaining oil and the coconut oil in another non-stick pan; add the fenugreek seeds and red chillies, and sauté for half a minute.

6. Add the marinated prawns, drumsticks and mangoes. Cook on medium heat, stirring continuously, till the prawns are almost cooked.

7. Add the strained curry and simmer for two or three minutes.

8. Serve hot with steamed rice or *Appam* (page 130).

56

nalli
nihari

Slow-cooking meat overnight till it drops off the bone requires patience and an unhurried approach to life. Much as one would love to indulge a yearning for that almost forgotten art, one instinctively reaches out for the pressure cooker!

ingredients:

• 500 grams lamb marrow bones (*nalli*) • 2½ tablespoons *Nihari Masala* (see below) • 2 tablespoons pure ghee • 2 medium onions, sliced and deep-fried till golden brown • ½ inch ginger, cut into thin strips • 2 tablespoons wholewheat flour • Salt to taste • 1 tablespoon lemon juice • 2 tablespoons chopped fresh coriander

method:

1. Heat the ghee in a pressure cooker. Add the *nalli* and the *nihari masala,* and sauté for two minutes. Add four cups of water and cook under pressure till the pressure is released eight times (eight whistles). This may take about half an hour.

2. Remove the lid when the pressure has completely reduced and transfer the contents to a non-stick *kadai*. Bring the mixture to a boil, stir in half the fried onions and half the ginger and simmer for two minutes.

3. Combine the wholewheat flour with six tablespoons of water and mix well till smooth. Add to the *nalli* mixture and continue to simmer till the gravy thickens. Add salt and stir in the lemon juice. Serve, garnished with the remaining fried onions, remaining ginger and the chopped coriander.

Nihari Masala

Dry-roast 4 tablespoons cumin seeds, 4 tablespoons fennel seeds, 12-15 dried red chillies, 2 tablespoons cloves, 5 green cardamoms, 3 black cardamoms, 25-30 black peppercorns, 4-5 tablespoons poppy seeds, 2 bay leaves, 1 blade of mace, 2 tablespoons dried ginger powder, ½ tablespoon nutmeg powder and 4-5 one-inch cinnamon sticks till fragrant. Add 4-5 tablespoons roasted split Bengal gram powder. Remove from heat and set aside to cool. Grind to a fine powder. Sieve the mixture and store in an airtight jar in the refrigerator.

57
braised lamb with spinach and leeks

Juicy lamb heaped with leafy greens in a simple, subtle sauce is both comfort food and fine dining fare. Serve it with steaming hot rice.

ingredients:

●400 grams boneless lamb, cut into ½-inch thick slices ●20 spinach leaves, stems removed ●1 medium leek, sliced ●2 tablespoons light soy sauce ●2 tablespoons fish sauce ●3 tablespoons oil ●½ cup chopped fresh coriander ●15-20 black peppercorns, crushed ●2 garlic cloves, crushed ●1 tablespoon brown sugar ●Salt to taste ●3 tablespoons lemon juice

method:

1. Place the lamb slices in a bowl; add the soy sauce, fish sauce, one tablespoon of oil, chopped coriander, crushed peppercorns, garlic, brown sugar and salt. Mix well and marinate the lamb for one hour in a refrigerator.

2. Drain the lamb and reserve the marinade.

3. Heat one tablespoon of oil in a non-stick wok; add the lamb slices and stir-fry for five minutes.

4. Add one cup of water and cover the wok with a lid. Cook the lamb over high heat till dry. Remove the lamb slices from the wok and keep warm.

5. Heat the remaining oil in the same wok; add the leek and stir-fry for two minutes.

6. Add the spinach leaves and cook for another thirty seconds. Add the marinade and half a cup of water.

7. Bring to a boil, lower the heat and simmer for five minutes; adjust the seasoning.

8. Pour the sauce over the lamb, drizzle with lemon juice and serve immediately.

58
stir-fried tofu with asian greens

Tofu provides the perfect palette on which to paint myriad flavours. Paired with barely wilted greens it is one of my favourite Oriental dishes.

ingredients:

●200 grams tofu (bean curd), cut into ¾-inch cubes ●2 tablespoons oil ●½ medium broccoli, separated into florets and blanched ●4 Chinese cabbages (pak choy), roughly chopped ●4-5 cabbage leaves, shredded ●Salt to taste ●2 inches ginger, grated ●½ teaspoon black pepper powder ●1 tablespoon lemon juice ●10 garlic cloves, chopped ●1 tablespoon soy sauce

method:

1. Heat one tablespoon oil in a non-stick wok, add the tofu and stir-fry for three to four minutes on medium heat. Sprinkle the salt, grated ginger, pepper powder and lemon juice.

2. Heat the remaining oil in another non-stick wok. Add the broccoli florets, Chinese cabbage and shredded cabbage leaves, and sauté for two minutes. Sprinkle a little water.

3. Add the garlic, soy sauce and a little more water and cook till the vegetables soften slightly.

4. Transfer the greens onto a serving plate. Place the tofu on top and serve hot.

59
ratatouille

The pronunciation (ra-ta-too-ee) itself tells you that 'stew' is too ordinary a word to describe this dish that celebrates the bounty from the vegetable gardens of Provence.

ingredients:

● 2 medium long brinjals ● 2 medium zucchini ● Salt to taste ● 1 tablespoon olive oil ● 2 medium onions, sliced into rings ● 4 tablespoons tomato purée ● 4 garlic cloves, chopped ● 2 medium green capsicums, cut into thin strips ● 3 medium tomatoes, blanched, peeled, seeded and chopped ● ¼ teaspoon coriander powder ● A pinch of cinnamon powder ● A few fresh basil leaves, shredded ● White pepper powder to taste

method:

1. Halve the brinjals and zucchini lengthways. Cut them again into thick slices.

2. Place the brinjals in a colander and sprinkle with salt. Top with a heavy plate and leave to drain for one hour.

3. Heat the olive oil in a non-stick pan; add the onions and sauté over low heat until translucent. Stir in the tomato purée and cook over medium heat for three to four minutes, stirring occasionally.

4. Rinse the salted brinjals and drain well. Add the drained brinjal and the zucchini to the pan.

5. Add the garlic and capsicums, and simmer for about five minutes.

6. Add the tomatoes, coriander powder, cinnamon powder, basil, salt and white pepper powder. Stir once or twice and cook over medium heat for about ten minutes, stirring frequently.

7. Adjust the seasoning and serve hot.

60
pan-fried mushrooms

Mushrooms have always been a favourite, and this bevy of beauties paired with colourful capsicums is a visual and gastronomical delight.

ingredients:

● 20-24 fresh button mushrooms, quartered ● ½ cup porcini mushrooms ● ½ cup oyster mushrooms ● 1 small red capsicum, cut into ½-inch pieces ● 1 small yellow capsicum, cut into ½-inch pieces ● 1 tablespoon olive oil ● 2 medium onions, cut into ½-inch cubes ● 3 garlic cloves, crushed ● 1 tablespoon soy sauce ● 1 tablespoon red chilli sauce ● ½ tablespoon vinegar ● ½ teaspoon dried thyme ● Salt to taste ● 8-10 black peppercorns, crushed ● 7-8 fresh basil leaves, roughly torn

method:

1. Soak the porcini and oyster mushrooms in lukewarm water for twenty minutes. Drain. Wash well and set aside.

2. Heat the oil in a large non-stick pan. Add the onions and sauté over medium heat till translucent. Add the garlic and stir-fry for a minute.

3. Add the mushrooms, red and yellow capsicums, and sauté on high heat for three minutes.

4. Add the soy sauce, chilli sauce and vinegar, and sauté for another two minutes.

5. Add the thyme, salt and crushed peppercorns. Remove from heat, stir in the basil and serve hot.

61
frittata with caramalised onions and roasted peppers

Brunch, lunch or dinner – any time is frittata time. The caramelised onions add a sweet note to the dish.

ingredients:

● 4 large eggs ● 2 large onions, sliced ● 1 medium red capsicum ● 1 medium yellow capsicum ● Salt to taste ● 1 medium potato ● 2 tablespoons butter ● ¼ teaspoon sugar ● 20-25 spinach leaves, chopped ● 8 black peppercorns, crushed

method:

1. Preheat the grill. To roast the capsicums, cut in half lengthways and remove the seeds. Place the halves, cut side down, on a baking sheet and grill until the skins blacken and blister. Remove, cover loosely with aluminium foil and leave to stand for ten minutes. Peel away the skins and slice the capsicums.

2. Bring three cups of water to a boil in a deep non-stick pan. Add the salt and potato, cover and cook till tender. Drain and set aside to cool. Peel, halve lengthways and slice the potato.

3. Melt the butter in a thick-bottomed non-stick frying pan. Add the onions, sugar and a pinch of salt. Sauté until the onions brown and caramelise. Add the spinach and continue to sauté for one or two minutes.

4. Whisk together the eggs, salt and crushed peppercorns in a bowl.

5. Arrange the potato slices overlapping each other, at the bottom of a non-stick frying pan. Scatter half the caramelised onions and half the roasted capsicums over the potatoes.

6. Pour the eggs over, even the surface, and top with the remaining onions and capsicums. Set aside for fifteen to twenty minutes so that potatoes absorb some of the egg.

7. Place the frying pan over medium heat. Cook, shaking the pan often, until the bottom of the frittata is lightly browned. Slide the frittata onto a large plate, turn it over and slide it back into the pan to cook the other side. Cook for another two minutes.

8. Transfer to a large plate and cut into wedges when slightly cooled. Serve immediately.

chef's note: You can divide the mixture between four individual ramekins and bake in a moderate oven till golden brown on top.

62
thai green curry with vegetables

Thailand's most celebrated dish is a personal favourite too! Who can resist a bowl of steaming rice doused in that silky green aromatic broth?

ingredients:

●1 medium carrot, cut into diamonds ● ½ small cauliflower, separated into small florets ●2-3 baby brinjals ●1 medium potato, cut into ½-inch cubes ● 5 lemon grass stalks ●1 tablespoon oil ●1 teaspoon lemon juice ● Salt to taste ● ¾ cup fresh Coconut Milk (page 159) ● 2-3 fresh basil leaves

Green Curry Paste
●10 green chillies ● 3 shallots ● 9 garlic cloves ● 1 inch galangal ● 3 inches lemon grass stalk ● ¼ teaspoon lemon rind, grated ● A small bunch of coriander roots ● 2 teaspoons coriander seeds ● 2 teaspoons cumin seeds ● Salt to taste

method:

1. To make the green curry paste, grind together the green chillies, shallots, garlic, galangal, lemon grass, lemon rind, coriander roots, coriander seeds, cumin seeds and salt to a fine paste.

2. Blanch all the vegetables. Tie the lemon grass in a piece of muslin. Crush it lightly.

3. Heat the oil in a non-stick pan; add the green curry paste and sauté for one minute. Add the blanched vegetables and lemon juice, and cook for three to four minutes stirring continuously. Add three cups of water and continue to cook. Add the lemon grass bundle and cook for three to four minutes till the curry is flavoured with the lemon grass.

4. Remove the lemon grass bundle and add salt and coconut milk. Simmer for one minute. Add the fresh basil leaves and take the pan off the heat.

5. Serve hot.

|rice|pasta|noodles|

63

kaju moti pulao

Less is more, they say, and this dish which is simplicity itself, is packed with flavour. Cover the *paneer moti* with silver *varq* for a special occasion.

ingredients:

- 20-25 cashew nuts • 1 cup grated cottage cheese • 1½ cups Basmati rice, soaked and drained • Salt to taste
- 3 teaspoons cornflour • Oil for deep-frying • 3 tablespoons ghee • 1 teaspoon cumin seeds • 2 black cardamoms • 2 cloves • 4 black peppercorns • 1 teaspoon turmeric powder • 1½ cups milk

method:

1. Add the salt and cornflour to the grated cottage cheese and shape into small marble-sized balls.

2. Heat sufficient oil in a non-stick *kadai* and deep-fry the cottage cheese balls till golden. Drain on absorbent paper. In the same oil, deep-fry the cashew nuts till golden. Drain on absorbent paper.

3. Heat the ghee in a non-stick pan; add the cumin seeds, cardamoms, cloves, peppercorns and turmeric powder. Sauté for one minute. Add the rice and mix.

4. Stir in the milk mixed with one and a half cups of water. Add the salt and bring to a boil. Add the cashew nuts; stir. Cover the pan and cook till done.

5. Transfer the rice onto a serving plate, garnish with the fried cottage cheese balls and serve hot.

chef's tip:

Fry one cottage cheese ball first, if it breaks while frying, add one tablespoon cornflour to the mixture.

64
jodhpuri vegetable pulao

Packed with dried fruit and nuts this *pulao* comes to us from the royal kitchens of Rajasthan. Serve it on a silver platter for added effect.

ingredients:

●1½ cups Basmati rice, soaked and drained ●12 small cauliflower florets ● ¼ cup shelled green peas ●5 tablespoons pure ghee ●1 teaspoon cumin seeds ●½ teaspoon fennel seeds ●15 cashew nuts, halved ●10 almonds, halved ●4-5 dried dates, chopped ●1 tablespoon ginger paste ●1 tablespoon garlic paste ●1 tablespoon raisins ●Salt to taste ●¾ cup yogurt ●½ teaspoon *garam masala* powder ●10-12 black peppercorns, crushed

method:

1. Heat four tablespoons of ghee in a deep non-stick pan. Add the cumin seeds and fennel seeds, and sauté till fragrant. Add the cashew nuts, almonds and dried dates, and sauté for a minute.

2. Add the cauliflower, ginger paste, garlic paste, raisins and salt, and sauté for another minute.

3. Add the rice and yogurt, and mix. Add two cups of water and the *garam masala* powder, and mix well. When the mixture comes to a boil, lower the heat, cover and cook till the rice is half-cooked.

4. Add the green peas and stir to mix. Cover and cook on medium heat till tender.

5. Sprinkle the crushed peppercorns and drizzle with the remaining ghee. Stir gently and serve hot.

65

erra saadam
(prawn fried rice)

Prawn Fried Rice, Tamil-Style or the Great Rice Make-Over! South India has a culinary tradition of stir-frying cooked rice with other ingredients to turn out delicious new dishes. And this one is a favourite.

ingredients:

● 450 grams small prawns, peeled and deveined ● 2 cups steamed Basmati rice, cooled ● 2 eggs, beaten ● 2 tablespoons oil ● ½ teaspoon mustard seeds ● 1 clove ● 1 green cardamom ● ½ inch cinnamon ● 1 bay leaf ● 2 large onions, chopped ● 2 garlic cloves, chopped ● 2 medium tomatoes, cut into small pieces ● ½ teaspoon red chilli powder ● Salt to taste ● ½ teaspoon turmeric powder ● 4-5 black peppercorns, crushed ● 1 tablespoon fennel seeds, powdered ● 2 tablespoons chopped fresh coriander

method:

1. Heat the oil in a non-stick pan. Add the mustard seeds, clove, cardamom, cinnamon and bay leaf, and sauté till the mustard seeds begin to splutter. Add the onions and garlic, and sauté for about five minutes, or until lightly browned.

2. Lower the heat and add the tomatoes. Cook, pressing the tomatoes with the back of the spoon, till all the moisture evaporates and the oil separates.

3. Add the chilli powder, salt, turmeric powder and one-fourth of the crushed peppercorns, and cook for a minute. Add the prawns and cook for five minutes, stirring occasionally.

4. Mix the powdered fennel, the remaining crushed peppercorns and a pinch of salt into the beaten eggs and pour over the prawns. Cook for another minute.

5. Add the rice and stir-fry for two to three minutes or until the eggs are cooked and the prawns are pink.

6. Garnish with chopped coriander and serve.

66
handi
biryani

You need to be a bit of a showman when you serve this dish. Slowly chipping away at the dough that seals the *handi* heightens the sense of anticipation. Then with a flourish, lift the lid to reveal the contents, which will perfume the air with the fragrance of exotic spices.

ingredients:

●1½ cups Basmati rice, soaked and drained ●4 medium onions ●A few saffron threads ●A few drops of *kewra* water ●Salt to taste ●2-3 green cardamoms ●1 black cardamom ●2-3 cloves ●1 inch cinnamon ●1 bay leaf ●1 medium carrot, cut into ½-inch cubes ●¼ medium cauliflower, cut into small florets ●10-15 French beans, cut into ½-inch pieces ●½ cup shelled green peas ●2 tablespoons oil + for deep-frying ●½ teaspoon caraway seeds ●½ tablespoon ginger paste ●½ tablespoon garlic paste ●4-5 green chillies, chopped ●1 tablespoon coriander powder ●1 teaspoon turmeric powder ●1 teaspoon red chilli powder ●¾ cup yogurt ●2 medium tomatoes, chopped ●½ teaspoon *garam masala* powder ●2 tablespoons chopped fresh coriander ●2 tablespoons chopped fresh mint ●2 tablespoons ghee ●1 inch ginger, cut into thin strips

method:

1. Chop one onion and slice the others. Soak the saffron in *kewra* water. Cook the rice in four cups of boiling salted water with green cardamoms, black cardamom, cloves, cinnamon and bay leaf, until three-fourth done. Drain and set aside.

2. Mix together the carrot, cauliflower, French beans and peas, and boil in three cups of salted water till three-fourth done. Drain and refresh under running water. Set aside. Heat sufficient oil in a non-stick *kadai* and deep-fry the sliced onions till golden brown. Drain on absorbent paper and set aside.

3. Heat two tablespoons of oil in a thick-bottomed non-stick pan and add the caraway seeds. When they begin to change colour, add the chopped onions and sauté until golden brown. Add the ginger paste, garlic paste and green chillies, and stir. Add the coriander powder, turmeric powder, chilli powder and yogurt, and mix well. Add the tomatoes and cook on a medium heat till the oil separates from the *masala*. Add the boiled vegetables and salt, and mix well.

4. In a *handi*, arrange alternate layers of cooked vegetables and rice. Sprinkle the saffron-flavoured *kewra* water, *garam masala* powder, chopped coriander, chopped mint, fried onions, ghee, and ginger strips in between the layers and on top. Make sure that you end with the rice layer topped with saffron and spices. Cover and seal with aluminum foil or *roti* dough. Place the *handi* on a *tawa* and cook on low heat for twenty minutes. Serve hot with *raita*.

67

kachche gosht ki biryani

This is Hyderabad's gift to the culinary universe. Unlike other *biryani*, raw meat is slow-cooked with the rice to produce a succulent, fragrant, layered delight.

ingredients:

●1 kilogram mutton or lamb on the bone, cut into 2-inch pieces ●2 cups Basmati rice, soaked ●2 two-inch pieces ginger ●20-25 garlic cloves ●½ cup fresh mint leaves ●A few saffron threads ●3 tablespoons milk ●2 cups yogurt ●2 green chillies, chopped ●2 teaspoons red chilli powder ●1 teaspoon turmeric powder ●Salt to taste ●4-5 large onions, sliced and deep-fried till golden brown ●5-6 cloves ●1 inch cinnamon ●5 green cardamoms ●1 black cardamom ●10 black peppercorns ●¼ cup *Potli Masala* (page 158) ●½ teaspoon caraway seeds ●½ teaspoon green cardamom powder ●2 teaspoons Hyderabadi *Garam Masala* Powder (page 158) ●½ cup chopped fresh coriander ●5 tablespoons pure ghee ●2 tablespoons rose petals ●1 teaspoon rose water ●1 teaspoon of *kewra* water ●Wholewheat flour dough to seal the pan

method:

1. Grind half the ginger and garlic to a fine paste. Cut the remaining ginger into fine strips. Chop half the mint leaves. Warm the milk slightly and soak the saffron in it.

2. In a bowl, mix together the mutton, yogurt, ginger-garlic paste, green chillies, chilli powder, turmeric powder, salt, one-third fried sliced onions and the chopped mint. Leave to marinate for one hour.

3. Bring five cups of water to a boil in a separate non-stick pan. Place the cloves, cinnamon, green and black cardamoms, peppercorns and *potli masala* in a piece of muslin and tie up in a *potli.* Add the *potli* to the boiling water. Add salt to taste, the caraway seeds and soaked rice. Bring to a boil and cook till partially done. Drain.

4. Arrange half the marinated mutton in a thick-bottomed non-stick pan. Spread half the rice over the mutton. Top with one-third of the fried sliced onions and ginger strips. Sprinkle half the green cardamom powder, *garam masala* powder and chopped coriander on top. Roughly tear half the remaining mint leaves and sprinkle over the rice. Pour half the ghee over the layers.

5. Add half the saffron-flavoured milk to the pan. Sprinkle with half the rose petals, rose water and *kewra* water. Repeat the layers once again. Cover the pan and seal the lid with the dough. Cook over high heat for five minutes, then lower the heat. Place the pan on a *tawa* and cook over low heat for forty-five minutes. Serve hot with *raita*.

68
mushroom pot rice

Clay pots, including our *desi mitti handi*, impart an earthy flavour to a dish, which is hard to replicate in any other cooking pan. The fragrance of mushrooms and spices that are released when the pot is uncovered will whet your appetite.

ingredients:

●3-4 oyster mushrooms ●10-12 fresh button mushrooms, sliced ●1 cup rice, soaked ●1 star anise ●2 tablespoons cornflour ●4 tablespoons oil ●1 inch ginger, grated ●2-3 garlic cloves, chopped ●2 spring onions, chopped ●2 tablespoons soy sauce ●¼ teaspoon MSG (optional) ●½ teaspoon white pepper powder ●Salt to taste ●2 cups Vegetable Stock (page 159) ●2 spring onion green stalks, for garnishing

method:

1. Boil the rice in three cups of water with the star anise until just cooked. Drain well, transfer to a clay pot and keep warm.

2. Soak the oyster mushrooms in hot water for fifteen minutes, drain and chop roughly. Mix the cornflour and half a cup of water. Set aside.

3. Preheat the oven to 180C/350F/Gas Mark 4.

4. Heat the oil in a non-stick wok; add the ginger and garlic, and stir-fry for half a minute. Add the spring onions and continue to stir-fry for a minute.

5. Add the soy sauce, oyster mushrooms, MSG, white pepper powder, salt to taste and vegetable stock. Bring to a boil, add the button mushrooms and stir in the cornflour mixture.

6. Cook for a minute or until the sauce thickens, stirring continuously. Pour the sauce over the rice, cover with a lid and cook in the preheated oven for twelve to fifteen minutes.

7. Uncover the pot, stir the contents well, garnish with the spring onion greens and serve hot.

69

shanghai stewed noodles

Spiked with chilli oil, this is the perfect meal-in-a-bowl. Keep the crunch in the vegetables so they serve as a counterpoint to the soupy, soft noodles.

ingredients:

● 200 grams noodles ● 1 tablespoon oil ● 6-8 garlic cloves, crushed ● 1 medium onion, sliced ● 1 spring onion, sliced ● ½ medium carrot, halved and sliced ● 4 fresh button mushrooms, sliced ● ¼ small cabbage, cut into 1-inch pieces ● ½ medium green capsicum, cut into 1-inch pieces ● 5 cups Vegetable Stock (page 159) ● 1½ tablespoons cornflour ● ¼ teaspoon MSG (optional) ● ½ teaspoon white pepper powder ● Salt to taste ● 1 spring onion green stalk, sliced ● 2 tablespoons Chilli Oil (page 159)

method:

1. Heat the oil in a non-stick wok; add the garlic, onion and spring onion with greens, and stir-fry for a few minutes. Add the carrot, mushrooms, cabbage and capsicum, and continue to stir-fry for a minute.

2. Add the vegetable stock, bring to a boil and add the noodles. Cook over high heat for two minutes. Lower heat and simmer for four to five minutes, or until the noodles are almost cooked.

3. Mix the cornflour with half a cup of water. Stir the MSG, white pepper powder, salt to taste and cornflour mixture into the noodles. Cook on medium heat for a couple of minutes or until the sauce thickens, stirring frequently.

4. Add the spring onion greens, drizzle the chilli oil and serve hot.

70
seafood pad thai

Street food in Bangkok is what I think of when I make this dish. The clang of metal against metal; clouds of steam rising from a hissing wok; coral prawns and yellow clams peeping through a mound of flat noodles.

ingredients:

●12 small prawns, peeled and deveined ●100 grams fish fillets, cut into 1-inch pieces ●8-10 mussels or clams ●200 grams flat noodles, boiled ●3 tablespoons oil ●5-6 spring onions, chopped ●5-6 garlic cloves, chopped ●1 medium green capsicum, cut into thin strips ●Salt to taste ●1 teaspoon soy sauce ●2 tablespoons brown sugar ●2 fresh red chillies, diagonally sliced ●5-6 spring onion green stalks, chopped ●3 tablespoons roasted peanuts, coarsely ground ●1 tablespoon lemon juice ●½ cup bean sprouts

method:

1. Pat the prawns dry with a kitchen towel. Open the mussels or clam shells with a knife and scoop out the meat.

2. Heat the oil in a non-stick pan; add the spring onions, garlic, prawns, fish and mussels or clams and green capsicum, and toss to mix.

3. Add the noodles, salt, soy sauce, brown sugar, and toss some more.

4. Add the red chillies, spring onion greens and most of the roasted peanuts one after the other, tossing after each addition.

5. Transfer to a serving dish. Sprinkle the lemon juice and bean sprouts, and top with the remaining roasted peanuts. Serve at once.

note:

To cook the noodles, bring seven to eight cups of water to a boil in a large non-stick pan. Add the flat noodles and cook till *al dente* (just done). Drain and refresh in cold water. Spread on a plate to cool.

71

spicy chicken fried rice with crispy basil leaves

The crisp basil leaves sprinkled on the rice is what gives this Thai dish its punch. Every forkful presents the crackle of fried basil which underscores the softness of the minced chicken and rice.

ingredients:

- 3 fresh red chillies • 2 green chillies • 200 grams minced chicken • 2½ cups cooked rice • ½ cup fresh basil
- 7-8 garlic cloves • Salt to taste • 3 tablespoons oil • 1 teaspoon fish sauce • 1 teaspoon sugar • 1 hard-boiled egg

method:

1. Pound together two red chillies, one green chilli, the garlic and salt with a mortar and pestle. Cut the remaining red chilli and green chilli into thin diagonal slices.

2. Heat the oil in a non-stick wok; add the basil and fry till crisp. Drain and set aside.

3. Add the chilli-garlic mixture to the same oil and sauté until fragrant. Add the minced chicken and stir-fry for three to four minutes. Add the rice and toss to mix well.

4. Add the fish sauce, salt and sugar, and continue to stir-fry for a minute. Sprinkle a little water and cook till the rice is heated through.

5. Add the red and green chilli slices, and mix thoroughly.

6. Halve the egg vertically and slice each half vertically into three pieces.

7. Transfer the rice onto a serving plate; garnish with the egg slices and crisp basil leaves. Serve immediately.

chef's tip:

You can also serve the fried rice on a bed of crisp fried basil leaves.

72

oodles
of noodles

Simple and heartwarming, this is our Pavlovian response to any situation calling for good food fast: an unexpected guest, a child to be placated or fed, a meal on the run, a snack between meals…

ingredients:

●200 grams noodles ●Salt to taste ●1 tablespoon oil ●2 spring onions, sliced ●1 small yellow capsicum, sliced ●1 small red capsicum, sliced ●4-5 French beans, sliced diagonally and blanched ●½ cup sweetcorn kernels, boiled ●2 teaspoons soy sauce ●2 tablespoons hot and sweet tomato ketchup ●1 tablespoon sweet chilli sauce ●¼ cup bean sprouts ●2 spring onion green stalks, sliced

method:

1. Boil the noodles in plenty of salted water. Drain, refresh in cold water and set aside.

2. Heat the oil in a non-stick pan; add the spring onions and stir-fry for a while. Add the capsicums and French beans, and stir-fry for a few minutes.

3. Add the sweetcorn and soy sauce, and mix well. Add the noodles and salt, and toss to mix.

4. Add the hot and sweet tomato ketchup and sweet chilli sauce, and mix gently.

5. Add the bean sprouts and spring onion greens, and mix well. Serve hot.

73

penne with creamy pesto and cherry tomatoes

Red, white and green, the colours of Italy and all things bright and beautiful, this pasta seems to say. And I agree.

ingredients:

● 200 grams penne (nib-shaped pasta), boiled ● 2 tablespoons cream ● 20 cherry tomatoes ● 1 tablespoon olive oil ● 2 garlic cloves, sliced ● Salt to taste ● 5-6 black peppercorns, crushed

Pesto Sauce
● ¾ cup fresh basil ● 3 tablespoons pine nuts ● 4 garlic cloves ● 2½ tablespoons olive oil ● ¼ cup crumbled Parmesan cheese

method:

1. For the pesto sauce, grind together the fresh basil, pine nuts, garlic, olive oil and Parmesan cheese till smooth.

2. For the pasta, heat the olive oil in a non-stick pan. Add the garlic and sauté till golden. Add the cherry tomatoes, penne, salt and peppercorns, and toss to mix.

3. Add the pesto sauce and mix. Add the cream and toss to mix. Cook for a minute and serve hot.

74
cheesy macaroni

This is the ultimate comfort food! Few dishes can satisfy a craving better than a carbohydrate-rich bowl of pasta laden with cheese.

ingredients:

● 1 cup grated processed cheese ● 300 grams macaroni, boiled ● 6 tablespoons butter ● 2 tablespoons refined flour ● 2 cups milk ● Salt to taste ● White pepper powder to taste ● 2 tablespoons fresh breadcrumbs ● ½ teaspoon crushed black peppercorns ● ½ tablespoon chopped fresh parsley

method:

1. Preheat an oven to 220C/425F/Gas Mark 7.

2. Heat two tablespoons of butter in a non-stick pan; add the flour and sauté lightly, making sure that it does not change colour.

3. Gradually add the milk, stirring continuously, so that no lumps are formed.

4. Add half the grated cheese and continue to stir. After adding the cheese, the sauce will thicken further, so add more milk to adjust the consistency.

5. Add the salt and white pepper powder, and mix well.

6. Heat two tablespoons of butter in a separate non-stick pan. Add the macaroni and toss to mix. Strain the sauce into the pan and mix gently.

7. Add the remaining cheese and transfer the mixture into a seven-inch square baking dish. Sprinkle breadcrumbs over the top and dot with the remaining butter. Sprinkle the crushed peppercorns and parsley. Bake till the cheese melts and turns golden brown. Serve hot.

| accompaniments |

75
sindhi dal

Traditionally served at breakfast, this quintessentially Sindhi dish should ideally be eaten with crisp *pakwan*, but it tastes just as delicious with rice, *roti* or *pav*.

ingredients:

• 1 cup split Bengal gram • Salt to taste • ¼ teaspoon turmeric powder • ½ teaspoon red chilli powder • ¼ teaspoon *garam masala* powder • ¾ teaspoon dried mango powder • 2 tablespoons oil • 1 teaspoon cumin seeds • 4-5 green chillies, slit • 8-10 curry leaves • 1 medium onion, chopped • ½ cup chopped fresh coriander

method:

1. Soak the split Bengal gram in three cups of water for about one hour. Drain and cook with three cups of water, salt and turmeric powder till just done.

2. Add half a cup of water to the *dal* if it is too dry and stir. Add half the chilli powder, half the *garam masala* powder and dried mango powder, and adjust the salt. Stir gently and cook over low heat for two minutes.

3. Heat the oil in a small non-stick pan and add the cumin seeds. When they begin to change colour, add the chillies, curry leaves, remaining *garam masala* powder and remaining chilli powder, and stir. Add the sizzling spices to the *dal* and mix well.

4. Garnish with the chopped onion and chopped coriander, and serve hot.

76
dal maharani

Every time I eat this *dal* I am transported back to my student days when I would return ravenous from college. A bowlful of cold *dal* straight from the fridge, with a couple of *paranthe* was like manna from heaven.

ingredients:

● ½ cup whole black gram ● 2 tablespoons red kidney beans ● Salt to taste ● 1 teaspoon red chilli powder ● 1½ inches ginger, chopped ● 1 tablespoon pure ghee ● 2 tablespoons butter ● 1 teaspoon cumin seeds ● 2 medium onions, chopped ● 10 garlic cloves, chopped ● 1 medium tomato, chopped ● 1 teaspoon *garam masala* powder ● ¼ cup cream

method:

1. Soak the black gram and kidney beans overnight in five cups of water. Drain.

2. Pressure-cook the soaked legumes in five cups of water with salt, the chilli powder and ginger till the pressure is released eight times (eight whistles).

3. Heat the ghee and butter in a thick-bottomed non-stick pan and add the cumin seeds. When they begin to change colour, add the onions and sauté till golden brown.

4. Add the garlic and tomato, and sauté till the tomato is pulpy and the oil separates.

5. Add the boiled legumes and one cup of water and bring to a boil. Add the *garam masala* powder and cook over very low heat for fifteen minutes. Stir in the cream and simmer for another five minutes.

6. Serve hot with *naan* or *parantha*.

77
methiwali arhar dal

Biting into a whole garlic clove may not be everyone's idea of fun, but for me it is one of the delights of this dish.

ingredients:

• 125 grams fresh fenugreek leaves, chopped • 1 cup split pigeon peas • ½ teaspoon turmeric powder • Salt to taste • 1 teaspoon grated jaggery • 1 tablespoon pure ghee • 6 garlic cloves • ¼ teaspoon asafoetida • ½ teaspoon red chilli powder

method:

1. Soak the split pigeon peas in two cups of water for one hour. Drain.

2. Pressure-cook the soaked pigeon peas in three cups of water with the turmeric powder and salt till the pressure is released four times (four whistles). Remove the lid when the pressure reduces completely and mash the *dal* well with the back of a ladle.

3. Add half a cup of water and jaggery, and bring to a boil. Cook for a few minutes.

4. Heat the ghee in a non-stick pan; add the garlic and asafoetida, and sauté till the garlic turns light brown.

5. Add the fenugreek leaves and sauté for two to three minutes. Add the *dal* and chilli powder and stir well. Adjust the consistency, if necessary, by adding water.

6. Serve hot.

78

dal lucknowi

Delicately spiced and enriched with milk, this *dal* evokes an era of royal repasts in the kingdom of Awadh.

ingredients:

●1 cup split pigeon peas, soaked ●2 green chillies, chopped ●½ teaspoon turmeric powder ●Salt to taste ●2 tablespoons oil ●1 teaspoon cumin seeds ●4 dried red chillies, broken into large bits ●5 garlic cloves, chopped ●A pinch of asafoetida ●1 cup milk ●2 tablespoons chopped fresh coriander

method:

1. Pressure-cook the pigeon peas and green chillies with two cups of water till the pressure is released twice (two whistles). Remove the lid when the pressure has completely reduced. Add the turmeric powder and salt and bring to a boil; lower heat and continue to cook for a few minutes.

2. Heat the oil in a small non-stick pan; add the cumin seeds, red chillies, garlic and asafoetida, and sauté till fragrant. Pour the sizzling spices into the simmering *dal* and mix well.

3. Stir in the milk and one cup of water and continue to simmer for two or three minutes.

4. Adjust the salt, garnish with chopped coriander and serve hot.

79

maa chole di dal

A perennial in our home, this *dal* speaks to the Punjabi in me. Like all comfort foods, its robust buttery flavours are eternally appealing.

ingredients:

• ½ cup split black gram, soaked • ½ cup split Bengal gram, soaked • Salt to taste • ¼ teaspoon turmeric powder • 1 inch ginger, chopped • 3 green chillies, chopped • 2-3 tablespoons pure ghee • 1 tablespoon butter • 1 teaspoon cumin seeds • 1 onion, chopped • 2 tomatoes, chopped • ½ teaspoon red chilli powder • 2 tablespoons chopped fresh coriander

method:

1. Place the soaked legumes in a non-stick pan with four cups of water, salt, turmeric powder, half the ginger and half the green chillies. Cover and cook, on low heat, for thirty-five minutes or till tender. Stir well, without mashing them.

2. Heat the ghee and butter in a non-stick frying pan. Add the cumin seeds and the remaining ginger and chillies. When the seeds begin to change colour, add the onion and sauté till the onion turns light brown.

3. Add the tomatoes and sauté till the tomatoes soften. Add the chilli powder and sauté till the oil separates.

4. Add the tomato mixture to the *dal* and mix well. Cook on low heat for five minutes.

5. Garnish with chopped coriander and serve immediately.

80

bhinda ni kadhi

Crisp *bhindi* swimming in a thick pool of golden yogurt - a summer favourite in our home.

ingredients:

● 15 ladies' fingers, cut into ½-inch pieces ● 3 tablespoons oil ● 2 cups sour yogurt ● 4 tablespoons gram flour ● ½ teaspoon turmeric powder ● 1 teaspoon red chilli powder ● Sugar to taste (optional) ● Salt to taste ● ¾ teaspoon mustard seeds ● ½ teaspoon fenugreek seeds ● 1 inch ginger, cut into thin strips ● 2 green chillies, chopped ● ¼ teaspoon asafoetida ● 2 tablespoons chopped fresh coriander

method:

1. Heat two tablespoons of oil in a non-stick pan; add the ladies' fingers and sauté till lightly browned.

2. Whisk together the yogurt, gram flour, turmeric powder, chilli powder, sugar and salt till smooth. Add four cups of water and whisk again.

3. Heat the remaining oil in a non-stick *kadai*; add the mustard seeds and fenugreek seeds. When they begin to splutter, add the ginger, green chillies and asafoetida, and sauté for half a minute.

4. Add the yogurt mixture and bring to a boil. Lower heat and cook, stirring continuously, till quite thick.

5. Add the fried ladies' fingers and simmer for two or three minutes. Garnish with chopped coriander and serve hot.

81

aamras ki kadhi

When in doubt, add both! This dish that calls for both unripe and ripe mangoes to make a tangy, sweet *kadhi* is ideal for summer.

ingredients:

• ¾ cup unripe mango pulp • ¾ cup ripe mango pulp • 2 tablespoons gram flour • Salt to taste • ¾ cup buttermilk • 1 tablespoon oil • A pinch of asafoetida • ½ teaspoon mustard seeds • ¼ teaspoon fenugreek seeds • 6-8 curry leaves • 2 green chillies, slit • ½ cup *boondi*

method:

1. Whisk together the unripe mango pulp, ripe mango pulp, gram flour and salt in a large bowl till smooth. Add the buttermilk and whisk again. Set aside.

2. Heat the oil in a deep non-stick pan on medium heat. Add the asafoetida, mustard seeds and fenugreek seeds, and sauté till the seeds begin to splutter. Add the curry leaves and chillies, and sauté for two minutes.

3. Add the mango pulp mixture and stir slowly to mix. Add one and a half cups of water to the pan and mix well. When the mixture comes to a boil, lower the heat and simmer for ten to fifteen minutes, stirring occasionally.

4. Add the *boondi* and simmer for five minutes till soft.

5. Serve hot with steamed rice.

82
appam

If *appam* are around, can a stew be far behind? Serve these lacy confections with a Malabar Chemeen Kari instead and you will begin to discover delicious combinations you have never explored.

ingredients:

●1 cup rice ●1 cup parboiled rice ● ¼ cup coconut water ●Salt to taste ● ¾ cup grated coconut ● ¼ teaspoon baking powder ●Oil to grease the *appam tawa*

method:

1. Soak both types of rice together in four cups of water for two to three hours. Drain and grind to a smooth paste adding the coconut water, as required.

2. Add the salt, stir well and set aside in a warm place to ferment for at least thirty-six hours.

3. Soak the grated coconut in one and a half cups of warm water; grind and extract thick milk. Add the coconut milk to the fermented batter to dilute it to a thick and creamy consistency. Mix in the baking powder and adjust the salt.

4. Heat an *appam tawa*; brush it with a little oil. Pour in one ladleful of batter and tilt the *tawa* all round to spread the batter. The edges should be thin and the excess batter should collect in the centre at the bottom.

5. Cover with a thick heavy lid and cook over medium heat for two to thee minutes. Check to see if the sides start leaving the *tawa*. The edges of the *appam* should be crisp and thin, and the centre soft and spongy.

6. Serve hot with stew or a spicy curry.

chef's tip:

●Traditionally fresh toddy is used to ferment *appam* batter. In the above recipe, the coconut water acts as the fermenting agent.

●A special cast iron *appam tawa* is used to make *appam*. However, you may use a small non-stick *kadai*.

83
sheermal

The Persian influence is evident in these saffron-flavoured flatbreads. They add a regal touch to a meal, the hint of sweetness mellowing the spices in the gravy they accompany.

ingredients:

●2 cups refined flour ●Salt to taste ●2 teaspoons sugar ●¾ cup + 3 tablespoons warm milk ●A few saffron threads ●2-3 drops of *kewra* water ●¼ cup pure ghee ●2 tablespoons butter + for greasing

method:

1. Sift the flour with salt.

2. Dissolve the sugar in three-fourth cup of warm milk. Soak the saffron in three tablespoons of warm milk.

3. Add the sweetened milk and two to three drops of *kerwa* water to the sifted flour and mix well. Add one-eighth cup of water and knead into a soft dough. Cover with a damp cloth and set aside for ten minutes.

4. Melt the ghee and add it to the dough; mixing it in well. Knead again into a soft dough. Cover and rest the dough for ten minutes.

5. Divide the dough into sixteen equal portions and shape into balls. Cover and set aside for ten minutes.

6. Preheat the oven to 240C/475F/Gas Mark 9. Flatten the balls on a lightly floured surface and roll out each ball into six-inch rounds. Prick the entire surface with a fork.

7. Grease a baking tray with butter, arrange the discs on it and bake in the preheated oven for eight minutes.

8. Remove, brush the *sheermal* with the saffron-flavoured milk and bake again for three to four minutes.

9. Remove, brush with butter and serve immediately.

84

moong dal puri

The ideal meal for a lazy Sunday. A few of these puffed up balls of fried dough with a little yogurt and a favourite pickle on the side, and you will want to stagger back to that armchair for a snooze.

ingredients:

●½ cup skinless split green gram, soaked ●1½ cups wholewheat flour ●3 tablespoons oil + for deep-frying ●1 teaspoon ginger paste ●1 teaspoon red chilli powder ●½ teaspoon coriander powder ●¼ teaspoon cumin powder ●¼ teaspoon *garam masala* powder ●Salt to taste

method:

1. Drain and coarsely grind the split green gram.

2. Heat two tablespoons of oil in a non-stick pan. Add the ginger paste and sauté for half a minute on medium heat. Add the chilli powder, coriander powder, cumin powder and *garam masala* powder, and sauté for half a minute.

3. Add the salt and ground gram and sauté for three to four minutes. Set aside to cool.

4. Place the wholewheat flour in a deep bowl. Add the salt, one tablespoon of oil and sufficient water and knead into a soft dough. Cover with a damp cloth and rest the dough for fifteen minutes.

5. Divide both the dough and the stuffing into eight portions each. Take each portion of the dough in your palm and spread it slightly. Place a portion of stuffing in the centre, gather in the edges and roll into a ball. Roll out into a three-inch *puri*.

6. Heat sufficient oil in a non-stick *kadai* and deep-fry the *puri*, one by one, till lightly browned. Drain on absorbent paper and serve hot with yogurt.

85

taftan

This is an aristocratic *naan* with a royal pedigree. Flakier and lighter than its more ubiquitous relative, it adds a touch of *tehzeeb* to a meal.

ingredients:

- 1¾ cups refined flour ●1 cup milk ●1 tablespoon yeast ●3 teaspoons sugar ●1 egg ●1 teaspoon salt
- 2 tablespoons yogurt ●1 tablespoon oil ●3 tablespoons ghee ●1 tablespoon onion seeds

method:

1. Warm half a cup of milk; sprinkle the yeast and sugar, and set aside till it starts to froth. Beat the egg.

2. Sift the refined flour with salt into a bowl. Make a well in the centre. Pour the fermented yeast mixture, yogurt, beaten egg and oil. Knead well to make a smooth elastic dough. Place in a greased bowl, cover with a damp cloth and set aside in a warm place for six to eight hours.

3. Punch the dough down, divide into eight equal portions and roll into balls. Brush with one tablespoon ghee and set aside, covered, for another twenty minutes.

4. Preheat an oven to 200C/400F/Gas Mark 6.

5. Roll out each ball of dough to a shape that is broad at one end and very narrow at the other. Then pull the narrow end gently so as to give it the shape of a teardrop.

6. Place the *taftan* on a baking tray, brush with ghee, sprinkle some onion seeds and cook in the preheated oven or in a hot *tandoor* for fifteen to twenty minutes, basting with the remaining milk and ghee once halfway through cooking.

7. Serve hot.

86
murgh missi roti

Purists may scoff at this non-vegetarian version of Punjab's most famous flatbread, but believe me, once tasted, these *roti* will be flying off the *tawa* faster than they can be rolled out.

ingredients:

●1½ cups minced chicken ●1 cup wholewheat flour ●1 cup gram flour ●Salt to taste ●1 teaspoon turmeric powder ●1 teaspoon *chaat masala* ●4 green chillies, chopped ●1 tablespoon dried pomegranate seeds ●1 medium onion, finely chopped ●2 tablespoons chopped fresh coriander ●1 egg ●1 tablespoon oil + for shallow-frying

method:

1. Mix together the flour, gram flour, salt, turmeric powder, *chaat masala*, green chillies, dried pomegranate seeds, onion, chopped coriander, minced chicken and egg. Add one tablespoon oil and just enough water to make a soft dough.

2. Divide the dough into equal portions. Grease your palms and roll the dough into balls.

3. Heat a non-stick *tawa*. Roll each ball in some flour and roll out into a thick *roti*. Place on the hot *tawa* and cook over medium heat on both sides.

4. Drizzle some oil around the *roti* and when one side turns golden brown, flip it over and drizzle some more oil, cooking the other side till golden brown. Serve immediately.

5. Alternatively, apply a little oil to the balls of dough and grease the worktop. With greased fingers, gently pat each one into a slightly thick *roti* and cook on the *tawa* as above.

87

tamatar ki chutney

A spoonful of this delicious chutney will make anything go down! Watch it disappear as it is scooped up with *pakore* and *paranthe*, slathered over kababs and chips, or engulfed in a mouthful of rice.

ingredients:

●7-8 medium tomatoes, finely chopped ●1 tablespoon pure ghee ●½ teaspoon cumin seeds ●A pinch of asafoetida ●1 green chilli, chopped ●10 curry leaves ●½ teaspoon red chilli powder ●¼ teaspoon turmeric powder ●1 teaspoon coriander powder ●½ teaspoon cumin powder ●½ teaspoon *garam masala* powder ●Salt to taste ●1 teaspoon sugar ●2 tablespoons chopped fresh coriander

method:

1. Heat the ghee in a non-stick pan; add the cumin seeds. When they begin to change colour, add the asafoetida, green chilli and curry leaves, and sauté for a minute.

2. Mix together the chilli powder, turmeric powder, coriander powder, cumin powder, and *garam masala* powder in one-fourth cup of water and add to the pan. Sauté for two minutes.

3. Add the tomatoes, salt, sugar and half a cup of water, and mix well. Lower the heat once the mixture comes to a boil and cook for ten to fifteen minutes.

4. Garnish with the chopped coriander and serve hot.

88

teekha nimbu achaar

Hot *lachcha parantha* with a dollop of butter and a smidgen of this hot and spicy *achaar*. Heaven!

ingredients:

6 large lemons, quartered and seeded ¼ cup salt ½ cup sugar 2 inches ginger, crushed 2-3 tablespoons red chilli powder 2 star anise, roasted 1 tablespoon roasted mustard seeds 1 teaspoon roasted fenugreek seeds 8 green chillies, chopped

method:

1. Place the lemons in a large bowl and sprinkle salt all over. Cover and leave to stand for one day. On the following day, toss the lemons in the brine.

2. Squeeze the juice of four quarters of salted lemons in a small non-stick pan. Add the sugar, ginger, chilli powder, star anise and three tablespoons of water. Bring to a boil, lower the heat and simmer, stirring continuously, till the sugar dissolves completely.

3. Pound together the roasted mustard seeds, fenugreek seeds and green chillies. Add to the mixture. Cook for one minute longer; remove from heat and set aside to cool.

4. Pour the remaining lemon quarters into a sterilised glass jar. Pour the cooled spice mixture over the lemons, pressing them down so that they are completely covered. Cover the jar with a lid and leave to stand for fifteen to twenty days for the pickle to mature.

89
spinach chutney (keerai chutney)

I came across this unusual Tamil chutney on a trip to Chennai some years ago and it has been on my list of favourites ever since.

ingredients:

• 250 grams spinach, roughly chopped • 1 teaspoon oil • 1 tablespoon skinless split black gram • 1 tablespoon split Bengal gram • 4 dried red chillies • ¼ teaspoon asafoetida • 1 medium onion, finely chopped • 1 large tomato, finely chopped • 2 green chillies, chopped • 4 tablespoons grated coconut • 2 teaspoons Tamarind Pulp (page 158) • Salt to taste

method:

1. Heat the oil in a non-stick pan on medium heat; add the split black gram and split Bengal gram, and sauté till golden brown.

2. Add the red chillies, asafoetida, onion, tomato and green chillies; sauté for five minutes.

3. Add the spinach, coconut, tamarind pulp and salt. Mix well and cook for two to three minutes. Remove from the heat and set aside to cool.

4. Grind to a fine paste and serve as an accompaniment to steamed rice, *idli* or *dosa*.

90
keri ki launjee

The melted jaggery coats the mango in a viscous deep gold syrup, to make a mouth-watering sweet and sour relish, which I am always hard put to resist.

ingredients:

●1 kilogram unripe mangoes ●3 tablespoons mustard oil ●¾ teaspoon fenugreek seeds ●4 teaspoons fennel seeds ●½ teaspoon onion seeds ●1 teaspoon coriander powder ●1 teaspoon red chilli powder ●½ teaspoon turmeric powder ●Salt to taste ●1¼ cups grated jaggery

method:

1. Peel the mangoes, cut them lengthways into quarters and remove the seeds.

2. Heat the oil in a non-stick *kadai* to smoking point. Lower the heat to medium, add the fenugreek seeds and sauté till they begin to change colour.

3. Add the fennel seeds, onion seeds, coriander powder, chilli powder, turmeric powder and salt, and mix well.

4. Add the mangoes and sauté for five minutes.

5. Add the jaggery and half a cup of water. Bring to a boil, cover the pan, lower the heat and simmer, stirring occasionally, for seven to eight minutes.

6. Remove from the heat and set aside to cool. Store in sterilised bottles when completely cold.

| sweets | desserts |

91
kesari indrayani

Too much of a good thing can be delicious! Succulent *rosogulla* steeped in a creamy saffron-flavoured sauce – sheer magic!

ingredients:

- A few saffron threads • 20-25 small *rosogulla* • 1½ litres full cream milk • 1 cup fresh cream • ¾ cup sugar
- ½ cup fresh pomegranate kernels • ½ cup *mawa/khoya*, grated • 8-10 pistachios, blanched, peeled and sliced
- ½ cup almonds, blanched and peeled

method:

1. Bring the milk to a boil in a non-stick pan; lower the heat and simmer till the milk reduces to half its original volume.

2. Add the cream, sugar and saffron, and cook till the sugar dissolves.

3. Squeeze the *rosogulla* to remove excess syrup and place them in a bowl. Pour the milk-cream mixture over and set aside to cool. When completely cold, place in a refrigerator to chill.

4. To serve, place a few chilled *rosogulla* in each bowl. Sprinkle the pomegranate kernels, grated *mawa*, pistachios and almonds on top and serve at once.

92
saeb aur
sooji ka halwa

The delicate flavour of apples transforms the plebian *sooji halwa* into a work of art. The apple slices arranged around add to its aesthetic appeal.

ingredients:

2 large apples, sliced thinly + 1 large apple, puréed ½ cup semolina 1 cup milk ⅓ cup sugar
½ teaspoon green cardamom powder A generous pinch of saffron 5-6 pistachios, blanched and slivered

method:

1. Dry-roast the semolina making sure that it does not brown.

2. Boil the milk with one cup of water in a deep non-stick pan. Add the sugar, cardamom powder and half the saffron.

3. Slowly add the semolina and cook, stirring, till fairly dry. Add the puréed apple and cook for two to three minutes.

4. Divide into four portions. Pack each portion tightly into a bowl or mould and turn the semolina out onto a serving plate.

5. Decorate with apple slices, pistachios and the remaining saffron.

93

mysore paak

Gold bars in a new bride's going away luggage? It's only Mysore Paak, which is traditionally presented to a bride by her parents! And you will see why – this honeycombed confection is precious!

ingredients:

- ¾ cup gram flour
- 4 cups sugar
- 2½ cups pure ghee

method:

1. Sift the gram flour twice. Heat the ghee in a non-stick pan and keep it hot over very low heat.

2. In another non-stick pan, cook the sugar with two and a half cups of water over medium heat, stirring continuously till it dissolves. Increase the heat and bring the syrup to a boil. Cook without stirring for about five minutes, or till it reaches a one-thread consistency.

3. Add half a cup of hot ghee to the syrup and stir; add the gram flour gradually, stirring continuously, to prevent lumps from forming, till the mixture comes to a boil.

4. Pour in the remaining hot ghee, half a cup at a time. Every time you add the ghee, the mixture should sizzle and froth.

5. Continue this process till all the ghee has been used up and there is a sweet roasted aroma.

6. Pour the mixture into a greased tray. Cool a little and cut into squares.

7. Separate the squares when completely cold and store in an airtight container to retain their freshness and crispness.

94

balushahi

This crisp doughnut-like *mithai* reigns over my memories of Diwali in Delhi as a young boy. The feel of the sugar dust on one's lips after each bite – sweetness and light!

ingredients:

- 1½ cups refined flour
- ¼ teaspoon soda bicarbonate
- 4 tablespoons pure ghee + for deep-frying
- 6 tablespoons yogurt, beaten
- 2 cups sugar
- 2 tablespoons milk
- 4-5 pistachios, finely chopped

method:

1. Sift together the refined flour and soda bicarbonate into a bowl. Rub four tablespoons of ghee into the flour mixture with your fingertips till it resembles breadcrumbs.

2. Add the beaten yogurt and knead into a soft dough. Cover with a damp cloth and allow it to rest for forty-five minutes. Divide the dough into twelve equal portions and shape into smooth balls. Take care not to overwork the dough. Make a slight dent in the ball with your thumb. Keep the balls covered.

3. Heat sufficient ghee in a non-stick *kadai* till moderately hot. Add the prepared dough balls and deep-fry on very low heat. If necessary place a *tawa* below the *kadai* so that the ghee does not get too hot.

4. Gradually the *balushahi* will start floating to the top. Turn gently and fry on the other side till golden. The entire process may take around half an hour to forty-five minutes. Drain on absorbent paper and set aside to cool for around forty-five minutes till they reach room temperature.

5. Heat the sugar with one cup of water, stirring occasionally, till the sugar dissolves. Add the milk so that the scum rises to the surface. Carefully remove the scum and discard.

6. Continue to cook till the syrup reaches a two-string consistency.

7. Remove the syrup from heat and soak the cooled, fried *balushahi* in it for two hours.

8. Gently remove the *balushahi* from the sugar syrup and place on a serving plate. Garnish with pistachios. Leave to stand for two to three hours till the sugar syrup hardens and forms a thin white layer on the *balushahi*.

chef's tip:

To check whether the syrup is of two-string consistency, place a drop of the syrup on your thumb and press your index finger on it and pull it apart. If the syrup forms two strings it has reached the desired consistency.

95
khubani ka meetha

Apricots and cream à la *Nizam*. The taste of this rich syrupy dessert lingers on the tongue and in the memory long after it has been devoured.

ingredients:

• 500 grams dried apricots (*khubani*) • ¾ cup sugar • ¼ cup fresh cream

method:

1. Soak the apricots in three cups of water overnight. Drain the apricots and reserve the water. Remove the seeds and crack them open to remove the kernels.

2. Boil one cup of water in a small non-stick pan. Add the apricot kernels and remove from heat. Soak the kernels for three minutes. Remove the skin and set aside for garnishing.

3. Boil the reserved water in a deep non-stick pan. Add the apricots and cook for nine minutes. Add the sugar and continue to boil till the sugar dissolves.

4. Remove from the heat and set aside to cool slightly. Reserve a few apricots and purée the rest.

5. Transfer the apricot purée to a non-stick pan. Add the reserved apricots and simmer for two to three minutes.

6. Transfer to a serving dish, decorate with fresh cream and apricot kernels.

7. Serve hot or cold. Traditionally it is served with fresh cream. It can also be served with ice cream or custard.

chef's tip

For the fresh cream, skim off the layer of cream which forms at the top of cooled, boiled full cream milk.

96
gajar aur khajur ka halwa

This is heartwarming food – the stuff that winters are made for. The dates add a natural sweetness and a Middle-Eastern exotic touch.

ingredients:

• 8-10 medium carrots, grated • ¾ cup dates, stoned and chopped • 1 tablespoon ghee • ½ cup sugar • 2 cups milk • ½ cup crumbled *khoya/mawa* • 4-5 cashew nuts, roughly chopped • ½ teaspoon green cardamom powder • 10-12 almonds, blanched and slivered

method:

1. Heat the ghee in a non-stick *kadai*. Add the grated carrots and sugar, and cook for about five minutes.

2. Add the milk and continue to cook for six to eight minutes.

3. Add the *khoya*, dates, cashew nuts and cardamom powder, and mix. Cook for ten to fifteen minutes or till almost dry.

4. Serve hot garnished with almond slivers.

97

mango
cheesecake

My silky tribute to the king of fruit! Fresh mango pulp is always best, but if like me you cannot wait till summer to indulge in this delicious dessert, use frozen pulp instead.

ingredients:

Crust

• 8-10 bran biscuits or digestive biscuits • 4 tablespoons butter, melted

Filling

• 2 cups mango pulp • ½ teaspoon mango essence • 1 cup milk • ½ cup condensed milk • 1 tablespoon cornflour • 1 tablespoon unflavoured gelatine • 1½ cups drained (hung) yogurt • 2 cups cottage cheese • ½ cup sugar, powdered

Topping

• 1 tablespoon mango jelly crystals • 1 mango, chopped

method:

1. Crush the biscuits to a coarse powder and place it in a bowl. Add the butter and mix well. Place the mixture at the base of a six-inch round spring-form tin lined with greaseproof paper. Press the mixture down lightly and place it in the refrigerator to set.

2. For the filling, heat the milk in a non-stick pan. Add the condensed milk and mix. Mix the cornflour with a little milk and add it to the hot milk. Cook, stirring continuously, till the mixture thickens. Set aside.

3. Mix the gelatine in a little water in a bowl and heat it in the microwave for one minute. Remove and set aside.

4. Place the drained yogurt in a bowl. Add the cottage cheese and whisk well. Add the mango pulp and mix again. Add the mango essence and the milk mixture and mix again. Add the powdered sugar and blend the mixture with a hand blender. Add the dissolved gelatine and blend again.

5. Pour the mixture into the prepared tin over the biscuit layer. Refrigerate for two to three hours.

6. In a pan, dissolve the mango jelly crystals in a quarter cup of water. Bring to a boil, remove from heat and set aside to cool.

7. Spread a layer of mango jelly over the set cheesecake. Chill until the jelly sets.

8. Remove from the spring-form tin and cut into eight wedges with a sharp knife dipped in hot water. Serve chilled, decorated with the chopped mango.

chef's tip

A spring-form tin is a round shallow cake tin with a removable base.

98

black forest gâteau

There are as many versions of this traditional German dessert as there are chefs. This is my favourite – simple and quick to put together, and absolutely scrumptious.

ingredients:

● 3 eggs ● 6 tablespoons sugar ● ½ cup refined flour ● 2 tablespoons cocoa powder ● 1 teaspoon baking powder ● ¼ cup milk ● 1 cup whipping cream ● Chocolate curls, to decorate ● ½ cup tinned cherries

method:

1. Preheat an oven to 180C/350F/Gas Mark 4. Line the base and grease a deep eight-inch round cake tin.

2. Beat together the eggs and sugar for eight to ten minutes, or until thick and pale. Sift the flour, cocoa and baking powder over the egg mixture and fold in gently, adding the milk as you mix.

3. Transfer the batter to the cake tin. Bake for thirty minutes, or until springy to the touch. Remove from the oven and leave the cake in the tin for five minutes to cool slightly. Turn out onto a wire rack, peel off the paper base and leave to cool.

4. Cut the cake in half horizontally and sprinkle each half with cherry syrup from the tinned cherries. Whip the cream until stiff.

5. Place the bottom half of cake on a serving plate and spread half the whipped cream over it. Cover with the top half of the cake. Use the remaining cream to cover the top and sides.

6. Decorate the gâteau with chocolate curls and cherries, and chill in the refrigerator.

Makes one 8-inch gâteau

99
strawberry panna cotta

'Cooked cream' doesn't sound half as romantic as Panna Cotta. For an impromptu special evening, whip up this dessert, decorate it with a few sliced fresh strawberries and wait for romance to fill the air!

ingredients:

● ½ cup strawberry crush ● 1 cup milk ● ¼ cup sugar ● 1 tablespoon unflavoured gelatine ● 2 cups cream

method:

1. Boil the milk with sugar in a deep non-stick pan. Cool to room temperature.

2. Mix the gelatine in four tablespoons of hot water and stir it into the milk.

3. Add the strawberry crush and cream, and mix well.

4. Pour into eight ramekins (small individual bowls) or moulds and place in a refrigerator to set.

5. Serve chilled.

100

tiramisù

A pick-me-up like no other – soaked in coffee and smothered with chocolate, it will have you flying on wings of delight.

ingredients:

•1 eight-inch round chocolate sponge cake •2 tablespoons + 2 teaspoons instant coffee powder •Marsala wine, as required (optional) •Cherry brandy, as required (optional) •3 egg yolks •¼ cup sugar •1 cup thick cream •½ cup powdered sugar •¾ cup mascarpone cheese •Chocolate curls, to decorate

method:

1. Slice the cake horizontally into two pieces. Cut into small rounds to fit into individual bowls.

2. Mix two tablespoons of instant coffee powder in half a cup of warm water and drizzle over the chocolate sponge rounds in the bowls. You can also use marsala wine or cherry brandy to drizzle over the chocolate sponge rounds.

3. Whisk the egg yolks with the sugar and one tablespoon of water in a double-boiler, or in a heatproof bowl over a pan of simmering water, till the mixture forms thick ribbons. Set aside to cool.

4. Whisk the cream with the powdered sugar till stiff and set aside.

5. Place the mascarpone cheese in a bowl and whisk till smooth. Add the egg custard and continue to whisk. Add the whipped cream and whisk till all the ingredients blend well.

6. Pour the mixture over the chocolate cake rounds in the bowls and level the surface.

7. Place two teaspoons instant coffee powder in a sieve and sprinkle over the cheese-cream mixture. Place the bowls in the refrigerator for one to one and a half hours, or till set.

8. Serve chilled, decorated with chocolate curls.

annexure

tamarind pulp:

Soak 75 grams tamarind in 100 ml warm water for 10-15 minutes. Grind to a smooth paste and strain to remove any fibres. Store in an airtight container in the refrigerator.

date and tamarind chutney:

Soak 75 grams tamarind in 100 ml warm water for 10-15 minutes. Grind to a smooth paste and strain to remove any fibres. Store in an airtight container in the refrigerator.

green chutney:

Grind together 1 cup fresh coriander, ½ cup fresh mint, 2-3 green chillies, black salt to taste, ¼ teaspoon sugar and 1 tablespoon lemon juice to a smooth paste using a little water if required.

mint chutney:

Grind together 5 cups mint leaves, 3 cups coriander leaves, 10 green chillies, 3 onions, and 3 inches ginger, to a fine paste, adding a little water if required. Stir in 1 tablespoon lemon juice, salt and pomegranate seed powder to taste.

coconut chutney:

Grind 1 cup grated coconut with very little water and salt to a thick paste. Heat 1 tablespoon oil and fry 1 broken red chilli, ¼ teaspoon mustard seeds ½ teaspoon split black gram and 5-6 curry leaves. Add the fried spices to the ground coconut.

hyderabadi garam masala:

Dry-roast together 100 grams coriander seeds, 25 grams black cardamoms, 20 grams green cardamoms, 20 grams black peppercorns, 20 grams cloves, 20 grams cinnamon, 15 grams bay leaves, 10 grams cassia buds (*kabab chini*), 10 grams mace and 10 grams nutmeg over a low heat for 8-10 minutes, or till fragrant. Cool and grind to a fine powder. When completely cold, store in an airtight container. Makes approximately 250 grams.

potli masala:

Mix 200 grams coriander seeds, 25 grams sandalwood powder, 35 grams dried vetiver roots (*khus*), 35 grams bay leaves, 20 grams dried rose petals, 25 grams black cardamoms, 30 grams cassia buds (*kakab chini*), 15 grams cinnamon, 30 grams lichen/stone flower (*pathar ka phool/dagad phool*), 35 grams Siamese ginger (*kulanjan /pan ki jadi*) and 25 grams ginger lily (*kapur kachri*) and store in an airtight jar. When required, tie a small amount in a piece of muslin and add it to the water to be used for cooking.

coconut milk:

Process 1 cup grated fresh coconut in a blender with ¼ cup warm water. Pass the ground coconut through a piece of muslin or strainer pressing firmly to extract all the juice, or first milk. Add ¼ cup warm water to the strained coconut to get the second, thinner milk.

chilli oil:

Cook 6 tablespoons of chopped dried red chillies in 1¼ cups of groundnut oil on low heat, for at least 10 minutes. When completely cold, stir in 2-3 tablespoons of red chilli powder and 1-2 tablespoons of sesame oil. Cover and leave to stand for at least 12 hours. Strain into a sterilised bottle and store in a cool, dark place.

chicken stock:

Boil 200 grams chicken bones in water for 5 minutes. Drain and discard water. Boil blanched bones with a roughly chopped carrot, celery stalk, leek, 2-3 parsley stalks, 6-7 black peppercorns, 5-6 cloves, 1 bay leaf and 10 cups of water. Remove any scum which rises to the surface and replace it with more cold water. Simmer for at least 1 hour. Remove from heat, strain, cool and store in a refrigerator till further use.

vegetable stock:

Peel, wash and chop 1 onion, ½ medium carrot, 2-3 inch celery stalk and 2-3 garlic cloves. Place in a pan with 1 bay leaf, 5-6 peppercorns, 2-3 cloves and 5 cups of water and bring to a boil. Lower heat and simmer for 15 minutes and strain. Cool and store in a refrigerator till further use.

red curry paste:

Pound together 10 dried, seeded, soaked and drained long red chillies, a large pinch of salt, 1½ tablespoons chopped galangal, 3 tablespoons chopped lemon grass, 2 teaspoons grated kaffir lime rind, 1 tablespoon chopped fresh coriander roots, 1 tablespoon chopped red shallots and 2 tablespoons chopped garlic with a pestle and mortar, to a smooth paste. Alternatively grind all the ingredients together in a grinder till smooth. Makes half a cup of curry paste.

sichuan sauce:

Boil 10-12 dried red chillies in 1 cup of water for 5 - 7 minutes. Drain, cool and grind to a fine paste. In a non-stick pan, sauté 10 finely chopped garlic cloves, 2 finely chopped green chillies, 2 finely chopped spring onions and 1 inch ginger, grated, for 1 minute. Add the red chilli paste and sauté for a few more seconds. Add 2-3 inches celery stalk, finely chopped, 3 tablespoons tomato ketchup, salt to taste and 2 teaspoons white vinegar, and simmer for 1 minute till the oil rises to the surface. Cool and store. Sichuan sauce will keep for 1 month if there is sufficient oil covering the surface.

tomato concassé:

To make 1 cup of tomato concassé, blanch 5 medium tomatoes in plenty of boiling water for two minutes. Drain and refresh in cold water; peel, cut in half, remove seeds and chop roughly.

glossary

Apricot	Khubani	Parsley	Ajmoda
Asafoetida	Hing	Ginger lily	Kapur kachri
Asparagus	Shatavari	Gram flour	Besan
Basil	Tulsi	Guavas	Amrud
Bay leaf	Tej patta	Lettuce	Salad ke Patte
Bean sprouts	Ankurit moong	Jaggery	Gur
Bengal gram, split	Chana dal	Ladies' fingers	Bhindi
Black gram, skinless, split	Dhuli urad dal	Leek	Bilayti pyaaz
Black gram, split	Chilkewali urad dal	Lemon grass	Chai ki patti
Black gram, whole	Sabut urad	Lemon rind	Nimboo ka chilka
Black peppercorns	Kali mirch	Lichen/stone flower	Patthar ka phool
Black salt	Kala namak	Mace	Javitri
Broad beans	Sem	Musk melon	Kharbooj
Broccoli	Hari phoolgobhi	Mussels	Seepee/shambuk
Button mushrooms	Khumb	Mustard seeds	Rai/sarson
Capsicum	Shimla mirch	Olives	Jaitun
Caraway seeds	Shahi jeera	Onion seeds	Kalonji
Cardamoms, green	Elaichi	Peanuts/ground nuts	Moongphali
Carom seeds	Ajwain	Pine nuts	Chilgoza
Cashew nuts	Kaju	Pomegranate seeds, dried	Anardana
Cassia buds	Kabab chini	Prawns	Jheenga
Celery	Ajmud	Prunes	Sookhe adu
Cherry tomatoes	Chhote tamatar	Refined flour	Maida
Chickpeas	Kabuli chana	Saffron	Kesar
Cinnamon	Dalchini	Semolina	Rawa/sooji
Clams	Seepee	Shallots	Chhote pyaaz
Coriander seeds	Dhania	Siamese ginger	Kulanjan/pan ki jadi
Cottage cheese	Paneer	Spinach	Palak
Cumin seeds	Jeera	Split pigeon peas	Toovar dal/arhar dal
Dates	Khajur	Spring onion greens	Hare pyaaz ki pattiyan
Drained (hung) yogurt	Chakka	Star anise	Chakri Phool/ badiyan
Dried dates	Chuare	Sweetcorn kernels	Makai ke dane
Dried mango powder	Amchur	Turmeric	Haldi
Dried vetiver roots	Khus	Vinegar	Sirka
Drumsticks	Saijan ki phalli	Walnuts	Akhrot
Fennel seeds	Saunf	Wholewheat flour	Atta
Fenugreek leaves	Methi	Yam	Zamikand/suran
Fenugreek seeds	Methi dana	Yeast	Khameer